FROM THATCHER TO CAMERON

The journey to Compassionate Conservatism

FROM THATCHER TO CAMERON

The journey to Compassionate Conservatism:
the collected Wilberforce Addresses 1997–2009

Conservative Christian Fellowship

edited by Kay Carter

First published in Great Britain in 2010 by
Biteback Publishing Ltd
Heal House
375 Kennington Lane
London
SE11 5QY

ISBN 978-1-84954-032-2

10 9 8 7 6 5 4 3 2 1

A CIP catalogue record for this book is available from the
British Library.

Set in Bembo by SoapBox, www.soapboxcommunications.co.uk

Printed and bound in Great Britain by TJ International Ltd, Padstow, Cornwall

CONTENTS

FOREWORD

This collection is a timely one – spanning as it does our thirteen years in opposition. It is a fascinating read. It stands as a great testimony to the reputation the Wilberforce Address, and the CCF itself, have acquired that such a diverse range of voices can be included – from within and outside the Conservative Party.

They range from Brian Griffiths, who played such a central role in Margaret Thatcher's government, to Canon Andrew White, talking about his reconciliation work in the Middle East; from Charles Moore to Bishop James Jones; from senior shadow ministers and former ministers to Rev. Katei Kirby; and from Ken Costa to no fewer than three leaders of the Conservative Party.

Looking through this collection not only highlights the invaluable contribution the CCF has made to debate within the Conservative Party, but it charts the changing course of the party itself.

We have certainly come a long way in the past thirteen years, but even in the very earliest Addresses there are plenty of indications of the themes that were to develop. We see this in Peter Lilley's focus on social justice as far back as 1997. We see it in William Hague's emphasis in 1998 on our needing to be the 'party of the whole nation', caring about the wellbeing of all of society, and his focus on the great social reformers in our party – Wilberforce himself, as well as Shaftesbury, Butler and Macleod. And we see it in Iain Duncan Smith's passion for social cohesion, and his emphasis on the twin themes of stable relationships and of localism – a passion which has been deployed since then with such distinction in his ground-breaking work for the Centre for Social Justice.

All these examples illustrate an important truth. What our party has done over the past four years or so is not to reinvent itself from scratch; rather we have developed important strands of Conservative philosophy which had always been there, but which had sometimes lain dormant and which needed drawing out, renewing and applying to modern problems.

That did mean changing our approach. Conservatives have long argued that the left talks too much about the state – and that's true. But we needed to recognise that the right has sometimes talked too much about the individual.

As William Hague noted in his Address, what really matters is what is in between the individual and the state. So today's Conservatives are not just concerned about the individual, but about the community; not just about the 'me', but the 'we'; not just about the market, but about society as well.

There is one other striking section from Peter Lilley's Address, delivered shortly after we had entered opposition those thirteen long years ago. 'The truth', he said, 'is that most of us who enter politics, whichever party we join, share some aims in common', particularly in relation to social justice. Despite this, he noted, 'there remains a sharp divide between the parties in our approaches, our analyses and our policies for tackling need'.

It is just such a realisation that forms the heart of the approach the party has adopted and developed much further in the past four years.

I believe that all mainstream parties are committed to four central, progressive aims that make up the vision of the good society and the good life. We all want to see, first, a society that is fair, where we help people out of poverty and help them stay out of it, for life. Second, we want to see an opportunity society, where everyone can, in the brilliant phrase coined by the shadow children's secretary, Michael Gove, 'write their own life story'. Third, we all want a society that is greener, and passes on a planet that is environmentally sustainable, clean and beautiful to future generations. And fourth, there is the safer society, where people are protected from threat and fear.

By and large, mainstream parties don't differ on those aims. What we differ on is how best to achieve them. Thirteen years on, it has become abundantly clear that Labour's approach has failed to deliver these shared goals. While notionally committed to progressive aims, Labour has delivered a country where the poorest are getting poorer and social mobility has stalled. The Labour government has failed to meet its own targets on carbon emissions, quality of life has gone down, and people today feel more at risk from the threat of crime – with soaring anti-social behaviour and violence against the person having risen. In short, thirteen years of the left have not delivered a fair society, an opportunity society, a green society or a safer society.

Our challenge today is not to abandon those aims but to succeed where Labour failed. We will do so because it is through Conservative means that these progressive aims can best be achieved. What are those means? Just as there are four principal progressive aims that we want to achieve, I believe there are four principal means by which a modern Conservative government can realise those aims.

The first – perhaps the defining – characteristic of the modern Conservative approach is a belief that we achieve progressive aims by giving people more power over their lives. Through decentralisation, accountability and transparency, we can make stronger and more responsible individuals.

The second means at our disposal is closely allied to the first – we understand that we must strengthen the institutions of civic society.

These include charities and social enterprises. But because there is such a strong link between social breakdown and family breakdown, the most important institution we must support is the family.

Third, progressive ends must include a plan for a new economy. It must be one that serves society – not the other way round. Social growth, environmental progress, quality of life as well as quantity of money – these are things economic progress must now deliver.

Fourth, we must understand that uncontrolled public spending and rising government borrowing does not advance our progressive vision – it threatens it. Fiscal irresponsibility means, at some point, the money will run out and there will be cuts in vital services. So we bring our Conservative instincts to bear and ensure that government lives within its means and delivers real value for money. But we also recognise that fiscal responsibility needs a social conscience or it is not responsible at all. So our approach to public spending control must both be fair and be seen to be fair.

And should anyone still doubt our commitment to putting progressive Conservative values into practice, the CCF have helped show the way in one other respect as well. In his Address in 1998, William Hague recounts the impression made on him during a ministerial visit to a church-based social action project. Today there are around 150 social action projects up and down the country, led by Conservative candidates and MPs. These range from job clubs to environmental projects, from young people's mentoring programmes to sports projects.

This work is not just confined to these shores. Each year scores of activists, MPs and candidates travel to Rwanda to work on a number of projects, from teaching English to training nurses. This year we expanded our work to include a group of lawyers working on legal reform in Sierra Leone, and William Hague and Baroness Warsi led a team to Srebrenica, home of the worst genocide in Europe since the Second World War.

The CCF itself has played an important part in helping us learn the lessons from existing social action projects so we can apply those to our own, and there are few aspects of the modern progressive Conservative Party of which I am more proud. Each one of these projects shows the difference we can make – and are making – even in opposition. And each one is a practical demonstration of the values that now guide us, and the values that will guide us if we are elected to government.

Over the past thirteen years, these Wilberforce Addresses have helped to chart our course in opposition. It is my hope that, over the next few years, future Addresses will be able to chart the difference which our progressive Conservative values can make in office.

DAVID CAMERON
JANUARY 2010

PREFACE

If we had been given a pound for every time someone said 'You can't be a Christian and a Conservative' we would both be a great deal wealthier today. The Conservative Christian Fellowship began in November 1990, when hostility to the Conservative Party among many Christians was close to a peak. The reaction to Brian Mawhinney's speech at a conference about Christianity and politics was typical. He was reported accurately as saying 'God is not Conservative' but his additional comments 'and God is not socialist and not Liberal' were conveniently ignored.

We felt the need for a forum that would help us to understand the relationship between our politics and our faith and would also, we hoped, enrich both. We founded the CCF while students at Exeter University. We had wanted to join with other Christians within the party to enjoy fellowship and discuss issues of common concern, but after contacting well-known Tory Christians we discovered that, beyond an ad hoc conference fringe meeting, no formal organisation existed and, at the tender ages of twenty and twenty-one, decided to establish the CCF.

Many people helped us in those early stages. Michael Alison, who had been parliamentary private secretary to Margaret Thatcher, became our first sponsor. Ken Hargreaves, then MP for Hyndburn, became our parliamentary chairman. Harry Greenway, MP for Ealing North, hosted our annual prayer gatherings, and Lord Griffiths of Fforestfach was a significant supporter from the outset. Jenny Stoker, who now works in David Cameron's correspondence unit, gave a great deal of time to ensure the production of our *Wilberforce Quarterly* magazine. The Wimbles family, Kevin McKenna and Frances Berrill gave masses of time to the prayer ministry.

In our early years our focus was perhaps a little too narrow and we concentrated primarily on the traditional concerns of Conservative Christians – the family and abortion. However, our horizons broadened with the help of the Listening to Britain's Churches process, which began in the late 1990s. Co-ordinated by one of our own trustees, Guy Hordern, it bought the fellowship into contact with more than 300 church groups of all denominations and concerns. We criss-crossed the country listening to church leaders and watching lay Christians help their neighbours to overcome every kind of social problem. LTBC helped the CCF become more interested in and more knowledgeable about a wide range of issues. The process ensured that we added a much greater poverty-fighting dimension to our mission. Contact with black majority and Catholic churches started to blossom, and has been taken to new levels with Elizabeth Berridge at the helm of CCF.

There have been many ups and downs on the twenty-year journey. One of the high points was seeing William Hague's Address to 5,000 Christians at Spring Harvest in 2000. We crossed a Rubicon that night in the Tory leadership's willingness to discuss issues of importance to the church. In the subsequent election of 2001 we distributed 250,000 newspapers to churches. Another important step was taken when the CCF took on responsibility for running the party's annual conference church service. No longer held inside the main conference hall, it now involves churchgoers from the host town or city and has become one of the best-attended and most vibrant events at Conference. The Wilberforce Address in the bicentennial celebrations of the abolition of the transatlantic slave trade was a further highlight, bringing together David Cameron, Bishop James Jones and some of our foremost black majority church leaders to address 900 people.

The development of Christians to take an active role in all levels of the party has been especially heartening. CCF's development programme for the under-35s has become a flagship event, helping Christians to equip themselves with the 'understanding mind' that King Solomon sought, as they approach involvement in public life.

We heartily acknowledge that there are committed Christians in all the mainstream parties, and through the work of Christians in politics we have been able to forge valuable partnerships with believers from across the political spectrum. It is disappointing that leading Christian organisations in public policy work have been slow to encourage Christians to join the political party that they normally support. If such groups had taken up this cause we would see many more Christians in parliament and local government. Keen to support those who seek to serve their communities in this way, we have run a number of 'engagement in public life' seminars, which have attracted people interested in positions from school governor to member of Parliament.

'God has put before me two great objects: the Abolition of the Slave Trade and the reformation of manners.' These words, written by William Wilberforce in his diary in 1787, and his example, provided the motivation for the founding of the Conservative Christian Fellowship. It was, and remains, our prayer that CCF and the Addresses that bear Wilberforce's name are worthy of him. He was a man who, motivated by his Christian faith, tackled the great evil of his day. It took him forty years to see the slave trade, and then slavery itself, outlawed. Wilberforce's moral clarity and his perseverance remain inspirational to us today. His example drives us into areas where the most vulnerable need a voice and assistance, domestically and internationally. The way that Wilberforce wanted to make goodness fashionable within the foundations of society must encourage us to support the role of the family, while his wish to pursue the end of the venality of political life and probity in commerce resonates strongly with the present age.

Aside from campaigns, causes and legislation, it was the people close to Wilberforce who mattered most. CCF sees the close group of people that nurtured Wilberforce and which he nurtured as a model for Christian involvement in politics. The so-called Clapham Sect that surrounded him was political, prayerful and pastoral. We give much thanks to God for sustaining CCF over these twenty years and for those political, prayerful and pastoral individuals who have been involved in the journey.

DAVID BURROWES MP AND TIM MONTGOMERIE
Co-founders, Conservative Christian Fellowship

THE WILBERFORCE
ADDRESSES

1997

Peter Lilley

For me, the name William Wilberforce evokes potent memories from my early childhood. For years these have lain dormant although, I hope, they have been seminal. Most summers, my parents would take me for a walk across the common a few miles from our home – ending at the Wilberforce Oak. There my father would tell me that beneath this tree the young William Pitt had persuaded another young man, called William Wilberforce, to devote himself to the abolition of the slave trade.

It made a deep impression upon me that two young men could set themselves such a noble ambition, that such a vile institution as slavery should ever have existed, and that, as my father explained, slavery had defaced every civilisation that ever existed. At least we could proudly claim to be the first to set about abolishing it.

Wilberforce's life is certainly an inspiring story with potent lessons for today. It teaches us that faith and ideas are more powerful than numbers. In Wilberforce's case, one man's faith was able to mobilise a whole nation's conscience. As the Old Testament says: 'One can chase a thousand. Two can put to flight ten thousand.' Wilberforce believed that human liberty should be fundamental to our whole vision of the world – and this belief is deeply rooted in

Christian principles. However, freedom is not just about achieving economic prosperity, as those on the right sometimes seem to suggest (though it clearly is the most effective system). Still less is freedom a luxury that can only be granted once basic material needs have been catered for, as the left often argue. Far from taking a patronising view that slaves would not be able to cope with liberty, Wilberforce believed the underdog needs liberty more than anyone else.

Josiah Wedgwood produced a wonderful 'tract' in pottery for the abolitionist cause. It shows a slave holding up his manacled hands, surrounded by the words 'Am I not a man and a brother?' Despite the chains, the black man is every bit the equal of his white brother. The true value of freedom is that it unites the human family in dignity.

You have asked me to discuss Conservative values and their relationship with Christianity and morality. Since you invited me to do so, we have suffered a chastening defeat and the whole topic has become of more pressing urgency. In the first place, we need to respond to our defeat with that most central Christian value of humility. We also need to re-examine our core beliefs to ensure that we rebuild ourselves on solid moral and spiritual foundations. We have to recognise that perception or, I would hope, misperception of Conservative values played a greater part in our defeat than actual policies. Finally, we have to decide how to respond to Tony Blair's attempts to identify his government with religious and moral values.

First, a little humility.

We were in government for an exceptionally long period. Particularly in the early years, we had to take some painful and difficult decisions. Indeed, government inescapably involves taking decisions that, even though they improve the general wellbeing, disappoint some people and upset others. Nonetheless this seemed to have little effect on our electoral fortunes. So we did not do enough to regain the respect, support and understanding of those who were upset by aspects of our policies.

Not surprisingly, people came to feel we were insensitive and unwilling to listen to their concerns. But as long as people feared Labour would undo our achievements, it did not seem to matter that they disliked us. We kept getting re-elected. Moreover, because our policies were recognised as being successful overall, our opponents made little headway in attacking them. So they increasingly attacked our motives and our values. They depicted us as greedy and selfish, and our policies as fostering greed and selfishness. We did little to repudiate this caricature, which became almost unchallenged in the media. Again, that had little effect while people feared Labour more than they disliked this ugly picture of Conservatives.

However, once Labour allayed those fears this accumulated dislike mattered a great deal, as we found on 1 May. The popular verdict was clear: we did not seem to listen to what people said to us; and we did not seem to deny what our opponents said about us.

I want to start the process of rebutting the caricature of Conservatives and Conservatism as essentially greedy and selfish. Of one thing I am certain: Conservative activists do not fit that caricature. Those I meet are quite disproportionately altruistic – they are deeply involved in community activities, charitable endeavour and church work.

By remorseless repetition, our opponents have established in the public mind the belief that Conservatism is a creed based on greed. Gordon Brown asserted this in typical form in his party conference speech: 'British qualities have been ground under by a crude free-market ideology based on the narrow pursuit of self-interest . . . the dogma that worships greed.'

It is a naked assertion unsupported by evidence, and a deeply offensive one. I know of nobody in any party who worships greed (though there are greedy individuals in all parties). Nor have I ever heard anyone promote 'the narrow pursuit of self-interest' as an aim of policy.

I hope none of us is tempted to stoop to traducing the motives of our opponents in such a way. I have always been taught that Christians should attribute to their opponents the highest motives compatible with their words and actions, however much we may disagree with their policies. It is time we asserted loud and clear that the whole Conservative tradition is based on the antithesis of what Gordon Brown asserts. It is based on a sense of obligation to others, particularly to those in need. My own personal Tory heroes are people such as Samuel Johnson, whose household was a veritable welfare state of frail and unfortunate people in support of whom he spent the bulk of his income. From my first days at the Department for Social Security, I took as my mantra his doctrine that 'a decent provision for the poor is the true test of civilisation'.

And there are countless others in the history of our party. Those such as Dean Swift, who gave away a third of his income to the poor and who scrimped and saved from the rest to found a hospital for the insane, or Burke and Coleridge, who based their profoundly conservative writings on deep Christian faith.

Much of our thinking about social justice today is informed by Disraeli's vivid descriptions of the 'two nations' of his time and his compelling appeal to the rich 'nation' to accept their obligation to alleviate the suffering of the poor. And let us not forget Lord Salisbury, who epitomised a sense of duty, honour and integrity.

Moreover, there is no conflict between this Tory sense of obligation to those in need and to our nation as a whole, and a belief in the free market. Adam Smith and Edmund Burke are perfectly compatible. Indeed, Smith said Burke was 'the only man who, without communication between us, thought on these [economic] topics exactly as I do'.

Samuel Johnson said: 'There are few ways in which a man can be more innocently employed than in getting [earning] money'. Of course, he added, 'getting money is not all a man's business – to cultivate kindness is a valuable part of the business of life'. Dean Swift knew that the creation of wealth came before its distribution. He gave it for his opinion that 'whoever could make two blades of corn grow . . . where only one had grown before would deserve better of mankind and do more essential service to his country than all the race of politicians put together'.

Of course we should not go to the other extreme and pretend that Conservatives have a monopoly of virtue. The truth is that most of us who enter politics, whichever party we join, share some aims in common. We all want to make life better for our fellow men, especially the least fortunate. We believe that the rich must help the poor; the healthy care for the sick; the strong support the weak. That is part of our common Christian heritage in this country, and it is wrong for any party to claim a monopoly of it.

However, although we all share common ends, there is no consensus on the best means of helping those in need. There remains a sharp divide between the parties in our approaches, our analyses and our policies for tackling need.

Labour's approach is still based on a hostility towards, and misunderstanding of, the free market. Nothing illustrates that more clearly than the sneering remarks of Gordon Brown that I quote above.

They see the market as based on selfishness and greed, generating poverty and inequality. They assume it is a zero-sum game, so that the wellbeing of some must have been attained at the expense of others. They believe unequal incomes reflect the arbitrary selfishness of employers rather than the relative scarcity of different skills, efforts and abilities. So they believe the state should intervene, not only to tackle need, but to impose a just and equal pattern of incomes. Indeed, an obsession with equality often results in concern for poverty giving way to the politics of envy. They fondly hope that the state can raise earnings ahead of people's productivity without destroying jobs, impose burdens on employers without reducing employment and penalise risk, effort and skills without affecting the amount of investment, enterprise and training.

By contrast, Conservatives see the free market as essentially positive. It releases and rewards human creativity and it allows people to prosper only in so far as they satisfy the wants of others. Over time it has enabled the vast majority of people in Britain to achieve a decent income.

Of course the market cannot directly help those who, through sickness, incapacity, caring responsibilities or temporary misfortune, are unable to participate in it. But it generates the wealth that enables us to meet the needs of those who cannot themselves participate in the market.

The obligation of a Conservative government, which believes in the free market, is twofold: first, to help those who cannot help themselves, and second, to provide a framework within which all those able to work can support themselves and generate the resources to help others.

In short: to help the helpless and enable the able.

Paradoxically, our success in raising general living standards merely intensified accusations that Conservatives do not care about the less well off, that we have let the poor get poorer or even that we have cut benefits. These accusations misrepresent our motives, our policies and our achievements. We do care. Our policies aim to help the least well off, and the results prove that they do work. The least well off have seen improvements over the past eighteen years.

I have always avoided sterile debates about how best to define poverty, but the people most of us normally think of as least well off are those who depend on benefits. Nobody should imagine that benefits permit a life of luxury, yet in most cases benefits are higher in real terms than in 1979.

We channelled an extra £1 billion a year into improving benefits for families with children. For example, benefits for an unemployed couple with two young children are now about 20 per cent higher than they were in 1979 (on top of inflation). Of course, a job is far better than benefits and we have been more successful in reducing unemployment than any other major European country. As a result, spending on benefits for the unemployed has been falling and now accounts for little more than a tenth of the total expenditure on all benefits. Far from 'cutting' benefits overall, the Conservatives met an 86 per cent increase in social security spending. The bulk of the increase in the social security budget has been devoted to help for pensioners and disabled people. We boosted our spending on the poorest pensioners by £1.2 billion a year. So the least well-off eighty-year-old couples are now entitled to at least £114 per week besides their rent and council tax.

We have also deliberately improved the scale of benefits for disabled people. In fact, we increased help for disabled people to four times the level under the previous (Labour) government.

Total welfare spending reached £90 billion: 36 per cent of central government spending. That means that, on average, the social security system costs every working person £15 every working day. On that measure the British people cannot be condemned as uncaring towards those in need. Of course, that level of spending has only been made possible because of the economic growth that our policies promoted.

It is significant that claims that the 'poor have got poorer' do not generally focus on benefit levels. Instead they largely relate to statistics for households with the lowest tenth of reported incomes. A growing proportion of these are self-employed, many of whom report low or even negative incomes particularly in the early years of setting up business. The other group that accounts for a large share of those on low incomes is the unemployed; most of this group return to work after a while.

Whatever their reported incomes show, those in the lowest tenth of incomes enjoy higher real living standards as measured by their spending – which is 30 per cent up in real terms compared with that of their counterparts in 1979. Over the same period the proportion of people in the bottom tenth of income owning consumer durables has risen enormously. For example, fewer than a third had a fridge-freezer in 1979. Now the overwhelming majority (84 per cent) do. Almost no low-income household in 1979 had a video. Now nearly three-quarters have one. Some 40 per cent had a car in 1979; now 57 per cent have one. To most people, the idea that well over half the group alleged to demonstrate ever-deepening poverty nonetheless have a car at least gives pause for thought.

In recent years, two issues provided ammunition for the enemies of freedom to fire at the free market. First, there has undoubtedly been a widening in the dispersion of earning power in recent decades. Across the developed world, the earning power of brawn has fallen behind that of brain. Some think this is due to technological change, others blame trade with developing countries, but whatever the true cause, a global phenomenon clearly cannot be the result of British government policy.

Too many commentators have wasted their energies (revealing a partisan bias) in blaming the most recent government rather than focusing their efforts on finding a solution to the problem. For if the earning power of unskilled workers falls or stays still at a time when benefits have generally been rising, this can make it less attractive for people with limited skills to work at all. This 'unemployment trap' would be worsened by sharp rises in benefits. For example, if the level of means-tested benefits were raised by £15 a week as the Rowntree Report suggested, not only would this cost an extra £6.5 billion, but an extra 1.2 million people would become newly entitled to benefit and be pushed into dependency.

The best long-term response to the problem of low earnings for unskilled workers is to improve their earning power. That means encouraging job seekers to acquire the skills, training, education, motivation and experience that makes them attractive to employers and able to command higher pay. That is easier said than done. It requires continuing reform within our schools, colleges, workplaces and benefit system. It will take a generation to come to full fruition, but it is well underway.

In schools, through the national curriculum, we increased the emphasis on technology and vocational skills. We tried particularly to improve the attainments of pupils of average or below average ability. Improved teacher training, systematic testing, the publication of school results and greater parental choice will all help raise pupils' attainments.

Already we have dramatically increased the numbers staying on at school or further education and going on to higher education. Only 20 per cent of children of unskilled parents stayed on at school after sixteen in the mid-1970s. Now significantly more than half do so. Which is why I find proposals to penalise families whose children stay on in education, by removing child benefit from 16–19-year-olds, so incomprehensible. Better skills, better training and better education offer the only chance of higher wages without higher unemployment.

Marketable skills are acquired not just through education. Indeed, most skills are acquired at work. At the most basic level what makes an employee more valuable to an employer are the habits of work, punctuality, motivation, adaptability and commitment. Those attributes are normally acquired, reinforced and rewarded in work. That is why we have put such store on encouraging people to take jobs. Because the longer people are out of work, the lower their earning power.

Our approach is threefold. First, to help and encourage people to take jobs, which is why we introduced the jobseeker's allowance.

Already, about two-thirds of unemployed people return to work within six months. We wanted to increase this, so our Jobseeker's Agreement is tailored to the needs of individual people and the efforts each unemployed person needs to make to get back to work. The right to benefits, however, is conditional on people genuinely trying to get back into work – as most are only too eager to do.

Second, we need to make work attractive relative to being on benefits. It is here that there is the greatest divergence between pro- and anti-market approaches. Those who believe market wages are at best arbitrary and at worst the consequence of malign employers see a minimum wage as the natural solution to low pay. Indeed, if I believed you could force up wages without reducing the number of jobs, I would happily impose a minimum wage. In practice a minimum wage would simply destroy low-paid jobs. As John Prescott pithily put it: 'Any fool knows that.' But it is worse than that. For the jobs that would be destroyed are exactly the kind of jobs that give people their first step up the ladder out of dependency. The lowest-paid workers tend to be employed in the most competitive industries. So a minimum wage would mean an employer could retain fewer workers and would force many firms to cease business altogether.

A minimum wage is also a very poorly targeted way of helping households with lowest incomes. A high proportion of those on low pay live in households with a higher earner. The Institute for Fiscal Studies calculates that a minimum wage will actually help households in the top third of the income distribution more than those in the bottom third. A much better approach is to let pay rates for each type of job find a level at which the number of jobs equals the number of people looking for work, but then give in-work benefits to ensure people are better off in work than out. For that reason we introduced family credit, which now helps more than 650,000 low-income families. That is why I continually improved it, and why we also improved the help we give people with their rents, to smooth the transition back into work.

The third thing is to give employers the incentive to generate more jobs – particularly 'starter jobs' – which will get the least skilled on the first rung of the employment ladder. Senior people in many companies began with starter jobs like these. Encouraging firms to employ more people means reducing the burdens and costs governments impose on employers. We have successfully reduced costs to British employers to a fraction of those on the continent. For the equivalent of every £100 of wages, a German employer has to pay £32 on top for tax, insurance etc. A French employer has to pay £41, but the British employer pays just £18.

Another issue that provided ammunition for the critics of free enterprise was 'fat cats'. When people who had been hired to work for a specific salary in a nationalised industry raised that salary as soon as their industry was privatised, it gave privatisation a bad name. John Major rightly condemned it. There is no defence of such behaviour from a free-market point of view. Their market value did not change overnight. They were not likely suddenly to receive tempting offers to move elsewhere. It was a different matter where new managers, who could command higher salaries, had to be brought in to manage privatised companies. That gave rise to little or no resentment.

Should the Conservative government have acted to remedy this abuse, and if so how? The true but uncomfortable answer is that this was a matter for shareholders. The way these monopolies' prices were controlled meant that the money came from shareholders, not consumers. In most industries, overall prices were fixed by a formula, and any unnecessary increase in the cost of directors' salaries could not be passed on in higher prices. So it meant less profit and dividends for the shareholders. If I had been a shareholder, I would have demanded to know why costs were being unnecessarily inflated in this way.

It is not, however, at all clear what the government could have done to remedy this public-relations disaster. Indeed, even this new government seems to have no plans to remedy the situation about which they complained so vehemently in opposition. The horse has bolted from the stable and it is little use debating how to shut the door, but it does lead on to a more general issue.

The freeing up of markets, restoration of incentives and changing technical trends over the past decade have enabled more people to gain large, sometimes huge, fortunes. How such people use their fortunes rightly or wrongly affects public feelings about the free-market system. In the United States they are more used to people making fortunes and less prone to the politics of envy, but above all, the cultural and religious climate in the US creates an expectation that the rich will plough back large portions of their wealth into their communities, the arts, charities, churches and universities. Indeed, one of the motives for success in America is to be able to do such things.

In Britain, we are wont to sneer at the flamboyant generosity of our American cousins, but we should surely aim to foster similar attitudes in this country. In his epistle to Timothy, St Paul wrote: 'As for the rich of this world, charge them to be liberal and generous.'

Wilberforce set as his second objective the 'reformation of manners'. His efforts had a tremendous impact in promoting a sense of obligation among the middle classes in Victorian England to use their wealth to benefit others. I am not keen on party politicians starting a similar crusade in this day and age, but rather than condemning the rich for their fortunes, the Church might well remind people that they are but stewards of their wealth.

Finally, how should Conservatives and Christians respond to Tony Blair's attempts to identify his government with religious and moral values?

We should certainly not impugn the sincerity of his religious convictions – they are genuine and admirable – but he is very unwise to allow his media manipulators to exploit his genuine faith as a cynical marketing ploy. Above all, we should rebut, and Tony Blair should repudiate, any attempt to portray New Labour as the exclusive embodiment of Christian values. No party has or should claim a monopoly of Christian faith, moral values or personal virtue.

I know many people are also concerned by the deliberate use of quasi-religious language in political speeches. My own view is this is more likely to bring New Labour into disrepute than to be a cause of offence to believers. Concocting speeches by the random permutation of agreeable buzzwords such as 'modernity', 'new', 'giving' etc. is an insult to the listener's intelligence. Including a few words with religious associations scarcely constitutes blasphemy, though it probably invites ridicule.

Indeed, the sanctimonious style of the Labour leader is already attracting ridicule. I am told, for example, that if you get through to the answer phone at No. 10, a recorded message says: 'Please leave your message after the high moral tone.'

More positively, Conservatives have a lot of ground to make up in our relations with the churches. It, alas, became fashionable in Conservative circles to dismiss the entire clergy as incorrigible lefties. A few of the clergy did echo Paul Tillich, the theologian, who said that 'socialism is the only possible economic system from the Christian point of view', but most do not.

It is true that many assume the free market is somehow tainted with greed, but that is simply because the moral case for free enterprise has gone by default. We have only ourselves to blame for that. It is time we put it right.

1998

William Hague

I was delighted to accept Tim Montgomerie's invitation to deliver this, the second Wilberforce Address, and I did so for two reasons. First, because I wanted to acknowledge – indeed to affirm – the work that Tim and the fellowship are doing to help the Conservative Party to change. Eighteen months ago, millions of people who share our values and our principles felt that they could not support the Conservative Party with their votes. We need to reconnect with those people, to persuade them that we share their hopes and their concerns for the future of our country.

As part of our wider Listening to Britain's Churches campaign, the Conservative Party, working in large part through the Conservative Christian Fellowship, is undertaking an ambitious and extensive consultation with Christian churches of all denominations throughout the United Kingdom. I mean this work to be taken seriously by the party and this meeting marks the launch of a new task force to make sure that it happens. The job of the Conservative and Churches Standing Committee will be to review and challenge the evidence collected by the Conservative Christian Fellowship through Listening to Britain's Churches, and to quiz members of the shadow cabinet about the future direction of Conservative policy. Gary Streeter will chair this group, which will meet for the first time later tonight.

I have invited a number of people outside the party, senior people in the churches and in Christian charities, to join the standing committee and I want to thank them for taking on this task. Their membership of the committee does not imply that they necessarily support the Conservative Party and, indeed, some are known to support our political opponents. This was a deliberate decision on my part. The Conservative Party needs to do more than listen to itself; it needs to listen to the whole of the British people. To use Rob Parsons's phrase, this will be 'listening with teeth'.

Already the CCF has begun an enterprising and demanding programme of work. Your chairman, Guy Hordern, has arranged meetings with more than a hundred leading Christian charities. In the New Year, Tim Montgomerie will spend three months with inner-city churches in some of the poorest parts of our country. Those areas may not have returned Conservative members of Parliament for decades, but the social problems and the human misery found in Peckham, Handsworth or Easterhouse matter not just to the people who live there, but they have an impact on the cohesion and wellbeing of our whole society, and they therefore matter to the Conservative Party. The Conservative Party must be the party of the whole nation. We are, as Disraeli said, a national party or we are nothing.

Listening to Britain's churches, and I want to stress that by that I mean listening to lay people and not just to clergy, will help us to renew that historic tradition of Conservative thinking and to regain the trust and support of the British people.

My second reason for wishing to accept your invitation was the fact that this Address has been named in honour of William Wilberforce.

While it would be wrong to claim Wilberforce exclusively for the Conservative Party, he was a man of Conservative instincts with a profound reverence for the institutions of this country, especially for Parliament. He changed the course of human history and did so for the better. He was a formidable politician and, perhaps you will allow me to say, a great Yorkshireman, born in Hull and member of Parliament for that city and later for the county itself.

William Pitt said of Wilberforce that he possessed 'the greatest natural eloquence of all the men I ever knew'. Gladstone recalled his 'silvery tones' in old age. Wilberforce could more than hold his own in debate, whether in the House of Commons or on the most rumbustious election hustings in Yorkshire.

He did not cut an imposing figure but could use eloquence, tact and withering sarcasm to tremendous effect. James Boswell, who stood in driving rain to hear Wilberforce speak in Castle Yard in York in 1784, wrote that he 'saw what seemed a mere shrimp mount upon the table; but as I listened, he grew, and grew, until the shrimp became a whale'.

His career has an epic quality: his friendship with Pitt; his conversion to evangelical Christianity; his relentless dedication to the abolition of the slave trade and slavery, regardless of the powerful vested interests ranged against him, or of the toll on his personal health. Long years of unsuccessful campaigning eventually bore fruit in the abolition of the transatlantic slave trade in 1807, and there is a sense of poetic fulfilment about his death, in 1833, just three days after the Emancipation Bill had finally passed through the House of Commons.

Though Wilberforce never held office in a government and though he had left the House of Commons more than eight years before his death, both Lords and Commons suspended business for his funeral. The Lord Chancellor and the Speaker were among his pallbearers. It was a tribute both to his achievements themselves and to the fact that Wilberforce, more than any other man in his generation, exemplified in his life how to translate a religious calling into political action.

After his conversion Wilberforce actually considered quitting politics for the Church, but after intense reflection he came to believe that God had a clear purpose for him. 'My walk', he said, 'is a public one. My business is in the world; and I must mix in the assemblies of men, or quit the post which providence seems to have assigned me.'

For me the story of William Wilberforce resolves better than any political textbook or theological tract the argument over the involvement of the churches in politics. I believe that it is right for Christians, both clergy and laity, to take an active part in political debate and political activity. While I make no claim to being a Biblical scholar, it does seem clear to me that the doctrines of creation and incarnation, which are central to the Christian faith, declare that God is engaged with and cares for the world that he has created and wants human beings to do the same.

When I was a government minister I saw at first hand some of the ways in which the churches in our country are trying to give practical expression to the Biblical command to love thy neighbour. I remember in particular a desolate housing estate in Penrhys, perched on a windswept hill above the Rhondda valley. The shops were closed and boarded up. There was graffiti everywhere. Most people on the estate were unemployed. You would be hard put to imagine a less fertile soil in which to plant the seeds of community spirit. Yet that is exactly what did happen, and that it did was due to the passionate, tireless work of the local minister, John Morgan. His efforts brought neighbours together and revived in that place a sense of common identity and purpose.

I went to that town to attend a church service where the children from the local school celebrated what they had done to help rebuild their community. It was an inspirational experience. I can think of no better example of Christian love in action.

That kind of work goes on today in schools, in inner-city projects, in housing associations, in work with disabled people, in support of broken families and in tackling the devastation wrought by drug and alcohol misuse. In many of this country's poorest neighbourhoods, the parish priest or the local minister will be the only professional person who actually lives there. The churches have valuable experiences from which politicians can learn.

So I have no objection whatever to lively debate, but what I do ask churches, and in particular some senior clergymen, to accept is that no politician and no political party has a copyright on scripture.

All too often, senior clerics have appeared to assume the moral superiority of a collectivist approach to politics and seemed ready to impute the most base of motives to those of us who hold to a Conservative view of the economy and society. Things have moved a long way since the Church of England was regarded as the Tory Party at prayer, but there are still many thousands of grassroots Conservatives who not only pray regularly but are actively committed to both the spiritual and the social mission of their local church.

For Wilberforce, Christian conscience was the wellspring of political action. He saw that slavery was an evil that stained Britain's reputation as the home of liberty and that it was his moral duty to fight for freedom and justice, even – perhaps especially – for those at the bottom of the heap.

Wilberforce was in many ways the ancestor of a noble line of Conservative politicians who championed freedom and justice, whose political ambitions were driven by compassion for their fellow men. The Conservative Party is the party of the Earl of Shaftesbury: the defender of poor children of the factories, the friend of the homeless, the founder of the Ragged Schools; the man for whom the statue of Eros, the angel of Christian charity, was erected at the end of Shaftesbury Avenue; the man who taught us about duty and compassion and responsibility to others.

We are the party of the great education reformers, of Forster, Balfour and Butler, who opened the school gates to the children of the poor; who believed that learning was not something reserved for the rich but was the rightful inheritance of us all.

We are the party of Iain Macleod, whose oratorical flair and political steel roused the conscience of both party and nation to the claims of our fellow human beings in Africa and Asia to determine their future for themselves.

It was not only for his work as a minister of the crown that we should honour the memory of Iain Macleod. He and his wife, Eve, were the driving force behind Crisis at Christmas. Macleod was generous with both his money and his time, and with Archbishop Ramsey he led the start of the pilgrimage from Canterbury to London in 1969 to rouse public support for the needs of the poor and homeless. Without his inspirational leadership and indefatigable support, Crisis at Christmas might never have happened.

The work of that charity today is as fine a memorial as any politician could hope for. In today's Conservative Party, we can see so far and stand so firm because we are standing on the shoulders of these giants. Conservative politicians and thinkers from Burke to Disraeli to Lord Hailsham have always drawn heavily on Judeo-Christian ideas about the freedom and dignity of individual human beings, about our mutual obligations one to another and our personal responsibility to care for our family and our neighbours.

That is not something that should cause any surprise. Just a few years ago, perhaps it is still the case today, students about to study for a history degree at Oxford were advised to start their preparatory work by reading the Bible. You cannot begin to tell the story of these islands without acknowledging the fact that for the past 1,500 years the culture, law and moral traditions of the British people have been Christian.

In saying that, I should also make clear that I welcome and value the contribution made by members of minority faiths to life in Britain. British Hindus, British Muslims and others are increasingly playing a full part in the mainstream of commerce, the professions, politics and the arts. They have religious and moral ideas, traditions of family and community, from which we all can learn. As part of Listening to Britain's Churches, I want to hear what those communities have to say. Respect for other religious faiths is no threat to Christianity.

But it is also true that Britain remains a predominantly Christian country. The Church still offers spiritual consolation to people in every city, town and village. The Church of England has a special place in our constitution. The way in which we debate political and social questions, the language we use, reflects Christian assumptions about right and wrong. Much of our great architecture, music and literature draws on the Christian capital of previous generations. You do not even have to be a regular churchgoer to find peace and spiritual reflection standing in the nave of York Minster, or to be profoundly moved by the beauty of choral evensong.

We Conservatives have looked less to political theorists for our ideas than to the history of our country. Our ability to set the political agenda for most of this century has depended on our capacity to understand and to reflect in our own policies the values and beliefs of the British people – what I have called 'the British Way'. That British Way itself draws heavily on the Christian moral tradition and so too do the principles that guide Conservative politicians.

Conservatives believe in limited government. I am sceptical of grand designs and promises of Utopia. The American statesman James Madison wrote that 'if men were angels, no government would be necessary. If angels were to govern men, neither external nor internal controls on government would be necessary'.

Children in Sunday school learn from the Biblical examples of Saul and David the truth that human beings are fallible and that power can be misused. A man who has power is inevitably subject to great temptation, even if, perhaps especially if, he believes that he is acting in a good cause. Throughout human history, and most horrifically in our own century, the pursuit of political paradise has led not to Eden, but to acts of appalling cruelty and to immense human suffering.

Even in a democracy there are risks that a majority may bear down on the freedom of individuals and minorities. So in any system of political organisation there need to be checks and balances to place limits on the untrammelled exercise of power. There is in addition a positive case for limited government. For most people politics is not the most important, or indeed anywhere near the most important, thing in their lives. Watch someone who is not a politician pick up a newspaper. As often as not, he turns first not to the front-page political story on which you have toiled for hours the previous day, but to the sports pages, or the fashion column or the crossword. Come to think of it, a sensible politician does exactly the same thing.

Lord Hailsham, writing more than fifty years ago, captured the point. He wrote that for the great majority of Conservatives, and I would add for the great majority of the British people, 'religion, art, study, family, country, friends, music, fun, duty, all the joy and riches of existence . . . are higher in the scale than . . . the political struggle'.

By limiting the role of government, we give people the opportunity and the responsibility to make moral judgements and to order their lives as they choose freely to do. From the moment that I first became interested in politics, I have not wavered in my conviction that the idea of freedom is central to the British Conservative tradition.

As over the past two decades I have thought about political ideas, I have found it reassuring to discover how freedom and freewill also lie at the heart of much Christian teaching. It is freedom that gives men and women dignity; freedom that allows diverse talents to flourish; freedom that inspires us to use the creativity with which we have been endowed; and freedom that gives us the opportunity to make ethical choices, to exercise our senses of compassion and of duty.

Josiah Wedgwood's cameo, which became the seal of England's Slave Emancipation Society, showed a black man kneeling in chains and the words 'Am I not a man and a brother?' For Wilberforce and his allies, freedom was an integral part of being human, the birthright of slaves as much as of kings.

It was a passionate belief in individual freedom and the need to defend it against the encroachment of the state that, more than any other single thing, drew me into politics. Today one of the things that still makes me angry is to see individual men and women in all their glorious diversity lumped together and categorised as a race or a class or an interest group. That is a simplistic and impoverished description of what our society is really like – the sociological equivalent of the Socialist Realist posters depicting life in Soviet Russia.

Freedom includes the freedom to own property. I think that this is certainly consistent with Jewish and Christian tradition, which acknowledges, most succinctly in the commandment not to steal, the validity of private ownership. Of course this is tempered with the qualification that those of us with property are under an obligation to use it wisely and with generosity and compassion for others, because the love of money or an obsession with material goods can corrupt the human spirit. I would add that the Christian idea of stewardship can give politicians of all parties important insights, not only into how best to conduct our own lives, but also into how best to shape public policy, on subjects such as the protection of our common environment.

Where there has sometimes been discord between the Conservative Party and high-profile churchmen is over the merit of an economic system based upon markets and free enterprise.

I suspect that few people in the churches today would argue in favour of full-blown socialism. The record of government planning and state control make that a difficult case to sustain. As the Roman Catholic bishops of England and Wales put it in their 1997 report *The Common Good*: 'Centrally commanded economies ... have been seen to be inefficient, wasteful and unresponsive to human needs. The market economy is the best system yet devised by man to create material wealth and to release people from poverty.'

In Britain today most people, including most church members, would acknowledge that an economic system based on the market is better at delivering the goods than one characterised by state intervention. What is less widely accepted is the moral case for capitalism.

'All right,' the critics say, 'the market economy works, but it has serious moral flaws. Capitalism fosters and rewards greed. It benefits the developed countries of the world at the expense of the poorest, and to believe wholeheartedly in individual freedom and in a capitalist economy is to deny the social nature of mankind.'

I want to deal with each of those points. In a free society, nobody is obliged to pursue riches as the highest priority in life. As T. E. Utley put it: 'Nobody is forced to extort the highest price for his labour or forbidden to embrace apostolic poverty as a vocation.' In any case, it is simply untrue to say that economic activity that is directed towards increasing personal earnings or accumulating profits necessarily springs from selfishness and greed. People are inspired by numerous different motives. For the entrepreneur there is the excitement of creating and sustaining a new business. For an employee there is the satisfaction of being able to provide adequately for his family and give the best possible start in life to his children. For others there is the opportunity to give money or time to improve the wellbeing of their fellow men.

Men such as Joseph Rowntree and Titus Salt used their industrial fortunes for philanthropic purposes, and while few people can afford to be generous on such a grand scale, similar acts of generosity go on today in practically every town and village in this country. Wesley's injunction to 'gain all you can; save all you can; give all you can' still rings true today.

Now, of course, many Christians in this country, perhaps including a number of people in this hall, will agree that, yes, capitalism and free enterprise have brought real material benefits to the United Kingdom and to other nations in the developed world. 'But', they will say, 'that ignores the harm being done to the poorest countries, at whose expense this has been achieved.'

The trouble with this line of criticism is that it is at odds with economic history. Despite the many problems we see at the moment in the developing economies of Asia or Latin America, the truth is that market capitalism has meant that, for the first time, people in those countries – which we used to class as part of the so-called Third World – can aspire to the material comforts and consumer choice that people in western Europe or the United States have taken for granted for several generations. A worker in somewhere like Hong Kong, whose grandparents lived or starved according to the success or failure of their meagre crop of rice, has gained a great deal from the advance of world capitalism.

Having made that point, and it is an important one, I want also to stress that any Conservative who holds to the tradition of Wilberforce or Shaftesbury should be seeking to help those millions of people in the world who are still in dire need. The Conservative tradition has at its best been neither little Englander nor little European, but international in its outlook. It is commonplace today to say that we live in a global village. Cheap air travel, modern telecommunications and, above all, the power of television to dramatise the most vivid and disturbing events in distant corners of the globe have transformed our mental picture of the world. For the Good Samaritan, Judea was a strange land. Today we are right to count Sudan and Nicaragua among our neighbours.

It is important to debate international development with the same intellectual rigour, the same readiness to learn from experience, that we apply when discussing domestic policies. We need to take account of the needs of the developing world when we negotiate the future of international trade. Protectionist devices such as the Common Agricultural Policy put up barriers against imports from poor countries. We need to make sure that aid is focused so that it goes to the people who really need it and not into the pockets of the local autocrat and his family. Here, the long practical experience of organisations such as Save the Children, Christian Aid and Cafod can be of enormous value.

We must be alert, too, to the risk that a benevolent gesture may have unintended but damaging consequences, as when emergency food supplies are misused, hoarded and end up by undercutting the local farmers on whose efforts economic revival depends. I know that there is particular concern in the churches at the moment about the burden of international debt and that many people see the chains of indebtedness as the modern equivalent of slavery. This is a subject for a speech in its own right, so let me stick this evening to three straightforward points.

First, I am proud of the work that John Major did to devise the Trinidad Terms and to put pressure on other developed countries to take the issue of debt seriously. Britain, under a Conservative government, did forgive the debts of the poorest. But things do move on and I want to pay tribute to the Jubilee 2000 Campaign for their work in raising public awareness of this issue. It is right for the Conservative Party both to be proud of what we did when in office and to acknowledge that further action on debt relief is now essential.

Second, gesture politics is not enough. A commitment to

reduce the burden of debt does not absolve us from the duty to ask rigorous questions. We must be sure that debt relief does not simply reward government corruption, and we must encourage developing countries to make sure that future loans are invested in ways that will generate economic growth and so help their own people.

Third, the Conservative Party under my leadership is going to continue to put the relief of debt at the centre of our policy on international development. Last week, Gary Streeter was the first politician to call for emergency debt relief for the countries of Central America, which have been devastated by Hurricane Mitch. After some dragging of feet, the government has agreed to take action. I welcome this and we will support the government in its attempts to continue the work, which we began.

Another criticism often made is that capitalism or the market economy is inimical to a sense of community, but this is to misunderstand how capitalism operates. Markets did not and do not operate in a value-free society, but in a society where both law and tradition are respected. Adam Smith himself assumed that moral considerations would govern individual choice. Values sustain markets. For a market economy to work, you have to have a generally accepted system of property rights, a framework of contract law and a medium of exchange recognised by all parties to a transaction.

The experience of Russia this century demonstrates with clarity how markets and community are interdependent. Soviet communism not only sought to control economic life but to strangle the institutions of a free society. The family was attacked, with Young Communists urged to inform on their parents. The churches were persecuted. Any encouragement to enterprise or thrift was stripped away. Every civic institution and value was undermined. It was the very opposite of the spirit of social enterprise that de Tocqueville observed in the infant United States, a spirit that built families, libraries, prairie schools and churches and which turned the Wild West into an oasis of prosperity and freedom. For Russia to prosper, a comparable social revolution is necessary. It is not just a matter of pulling economic levers, there also needs to be an acceptance of diversity, pluralism and the rule of law. The success of our own economy depends upon Judeo-Christian values and voluntary institutions as much as it depends upon the level of taxation or the liberalisation of trade.

Conservatives believe in freedom, but we also believe in responsibility. A prime reason for our scepticism about government intervention and regulation is that it deprives people of their right to make moral choices. That is bad for the individual concerned and bad for society as a whole. In a modern society, there is a legitimate role for the state. I spent one of the most rewarding years of my life as minister for disabled people. Their courage and determination was an inspiration to me; in many cases they were blessed with support from a loving family or from the generosity of volunteers. But I saw too that it was not enough to leave everything to voluntary action and I argued successfully for the government to outlaw discrimination and improve disability benefits. Action by the state helped disabled people to help themselves.

Since the public wants and needs services – schools, hospitals, the police – I also accept and believe that it is necessary for government to levy taxes. Necessary, yes, but there is nothing particularly virtuous about taxation. Taxation ultimately is a matter of coercion, not of giving. We are familiar with the economic case for lower taxes: that they provide incentives to create wealth, to provide new jobs, to increase investment. Individuals and companies are better able than civil servants or politicians to decide how to spend their money in order to get the best possible return. The experience of the Thatcher government here and of the Reagan administration in the United States is that the surest route to prosperity is to let money fructify in the pockets of the people.

However, there is also a powerful moral case for lower taxes. It is partly a straightforward matter of justice: the money that someone earns in return for his labour should be his to own and his to spend. Taxation, like marriage in the words of the Book of Common Prayer, is something not to be entered into lightly or wantonly, but soberly and advisedly, with a proper recognition by government that in levying taxation it is not just taking someone's property, but is also depriving that citizen of the right and the responsibility to choose how to spend his earnings. I believe that it is no accident that in the United States, where the culture of enterprise, free markets and low taxes is most strongly entrenched, there is also a culture of giving, to charities, to churches, to education and to the arts.

I recognise the benefits that the modern welfare state has brought to our own country, and I do not wish, nor do I intend to try, to turn back the clock to the days before the war, when many people lived in fear that they would not be able to have medical treatment when they were ill or a decent income in their old age because they didn't have the money. However, we need to recognise that when the state takes over responsibility for decisions about healthcare, schooling, pensions and other welfare provision, a price is paid in a diminished sense of civic obligation and personal responsibility. Too many people in our country now believe that they have completed their civic duty along with their tax return. Cutting taxes, and in particular taxes on earnings, is part of the process of rekindling a sense of personal responsibility, of trying to create a welfare society and not just a welfare state.

A healthy and cohesive society depends crucially on the health of the institution of the family. Edmund Burke wrote: 'No cold relation can be a zealous citizen.' The family is the building block of institutional loyalty and affection. Every member of Parliament knows from his constituency postbag and his weekly advice bureau that many of the problems that land on our desks, though ostensibly about debt or housing or social security benefits or special educational needs, derive originally from the breakdown of a family. It is commonplace to acknowledge that family life in Britain today is more complicated and more varied than in my parents' or grandparents' generation. That is a fact with which both politicians and the churches must deal. There are thousands of parents who have been abandoned by partners or spouses. To them we owe respect and support in bringing up their children. There are others who have taken a decision to lead their lives in a way very different from a traditional family pattern. In a free society that is their choice and tolerance is one of the hallmarks of a mature and decent society.

Important though those points are, the central truth in any discussion of family policy is surely this: it is the institution of marriage, the lifelong and exclusive commitment of one man and one woman to each other, which provides the best hope for stable family life and for the upbringing of children. In report after report, in this country and elsewhere, sociological research is bearing out the truth which common sense has always known. Children are hurt by divorce. Families need both fathers and mothers. One income can rarely support two households. Government figures show how divorce and single parenthood have added to welfare dependency.

It is not for any politician to berate or condemn. Those official statistics chart an ocean of human grief. The Conservative Party is not against single parents; it is strongly and unreservedly for the institution of marriage. Many of the single parents who come to my constituency surgery, people struggling hard to bring up their children in the best way they can, would actually agree with that. People who have themselves suffered the agony of marital breakdown and divorce want others to succeed. In framing policies for the future, I believe that politicians have a duty to seek ways to strengthen marriage, to strengthen family life and to provide a better chance for future generations of children.

The Labour government recently published its Green Paper on family policy. Some things in it, like encouragement for the role of grandparents, are sensible and we shall support them. Others, like asking registrars or health visitors to act as a kind of state vicar, are pretty risible. What is utterly dismaying is how Labour has ignored the central problem and shied away from using the tax and benefit system to provide support for marriage. Indeed, Jack Straw's Ministerial Committee on Family Policy was expressly forbidden to consider how the tax system might be so used.

One of the few consolations of opposition is that the Conservative Party is free to think. We can look back with the benefit of hindsight on our record in office and come to a clear-eyed assessment of our successes and failures. In retrospect, I still believe that we were right to introduce independent taxation for men and women, but that we made a mistake in not coupling this, as Nigel Lawson had originally intended, with a system of transferable tax allowances between husbands and wives. You may agree that it is also a pity that the churches did not speak out loudly in favour of transferability before those decisions were made. With hindsight too, we were wrong to make such significant cuts to the married couple's tax allowance without putting anything else in its place.

Of course there were arguments in favour of what we did, arguments that, because of the need to reduce government borrowing, looked good at the time. But partly because of those decisions, many people in the country came to believe that the Conservative Party was no longer interested in supporting families or the institution of marriage. At the general election we put forward a first-rate policy: a transferable tax allowance available to married couples where one of them was working and the other stayed at home to care for young children or an elderly relative. It was a good policy but it carried little credibility with the electorate because, in the light of what had happened before, people did not take our commitment seriously.

Now Labour is intent on getting rid of the married couple's allowance altogether and with it the last recognition of marriage within the tax system. On top of that Labour seems likely to press ahead with plans to tax child benefit, treating husbands and wives as a single unit for tax purposes in that respect only, while refusing point blank to consider married couples as a single unit when it comes to the potential transfer of personal tax allowances. That would be utterly wrong.

I do not believe that the tax system should be neutral about marriage. A top priority for Conservatives now is to develop tax and benefit policies that demonstrate clearly our commitment to strengthen families and to marriage. I have therefore asked my deputy, Peter Lilley, to lead a Conservative Party task force on family policy, and he will be joined in this work by other senior members of my shadow cabinet team. The remit of this task force is to consider every aspect of public policy in terms of how it affects family and marriage and to bring forward ideas that we can include in our manifesto at the next general election. Labour banned Jack Straw's working group from even looking at tax policy; tax policy will be high on the agenda for our party's task force. I have also agreed with Peter that his group should study the work of the many charities and voluntary organisations already active in helping to support families. He will, I know, want the churches to give us the benefit of their views.

Conservatives support the family as the nursery of responsibility and independence. We also stand for local institutions, for the little platoons that Burke described. To talk about society in terms of a relationship between, on the one hand, atomised individuals and, on the other, either a benevolent or an overbearing state seems to me to caricature reality. The truth is that we are a nation of individuals and families and football supporters and choral societies and pigeon fanciers and shopkeepers and classic car owners and charities, even of political parties.

We are also a nation of churches, churches that are themselves influential voluntary organisations and whose lay members are also involved in the work of a myriad of other groups. As a member of Parliament you enjoy the privilege of being able to take an interest in the innumerable different organisations and professions in your patch. One of the things I find is that I may meet a woman who is a Conservative branch chairman in one village, a school governor in another, serves on the county committee for a charity and is singing in the church choir at the civic service.

Each one of us belongs to many different communities, some defined by place, others by activity. The number and variety of voluntary organisations is surely one of the most admirable characteristics of British society. I believe that we need to look for ways to harness the energy and the spontaneity of voluntary organisations in tackling our country's social problems. A great deal is already being done, not least by churches and the various charities that they support. Many of those groups are represented here this evening. Some are working to heal racial tension in our inner cities; others, such as Life, are supporting young women through difficult pregnancies, giving them the confidence to choose not to have an abortion; others still work on behalf of homeless people or those who are mentally ill, or give help to alcoholics and drug misusers.

In renewing our party's policies, I want to consider how we can build on our experience of paying for public services out of our taxes but having them delivered by voluntary organisations. My criticism of a document like *Faith in the City* or of the comments of people like Bishop David Sheppard is that they place too much faith in the effectiveness and the impartiality of state intervention. A government rule book, drawn up to cover all eventualities, cannot provide the scope for flexibility and innovation we need. Too often, and as a former social security minister I speak with some feeling on this subject, the rules fail to provide for some particular deserving case while apparently rewarding those who are abusing the system. We must find ways to help people who are in need, recognising the differences between individual cases, without recreating all the faults of the old Victorian Poor Law.

Let me suggest one example. The plight of children in local authority care and of young people leaving care is a silent scandal. These children are often both materially and emotionally deprived. Many bear the scars of traumatic home backgrounds. Society – you and I – has the responsibility to act as their parents and while I do not for one minute doubt the good intentions of local authority social services departments, the truth is that we are failing these young people. Young people leaving care are often simply unable to cope with the isolation and practical demands of living on their own. According to the charity NCH, between half and four-fifths of those leaving care are unemployed. Nearly 40 per cent of young prisoners have been in care and youngsters leaving care are greatly over-represented in the numbers of homeless people.

While there is much in the government's response to the Utting report that we can welcome and support, I want to explore whether we should be bolder in addressing this social problem. In many places, churches and charities are already giving help to these young people. Should we now consider transferring from social services departments all or part of their responsibility under the Children Act to 'advise, assist and befriend' youngsters leaving care? Might voluntary organisations, perhaps church led, be among those best equipped to carry out some of these tasks, be more responsive, better able to tailor their help to the individual needs of each young man or woman needing support? Could we be more imaginative still and consider giving the voluntary sector a greater role in running this country's children's homes? Is there perhaps a role for the churches here as well?

These subjects are too important to be considered lightly. Matters like the training and vetting of staff would have to be thought through in detail, but I mean this as a positive proposal. If church leaders are serious about showing their commitment to the needy through political action then perhaps a redefinition of the partnership between the voluntary sector and the state is one of the ways forward. I want to hear the views of the churches on this. The Conservative Party, including the Conservative Christian Fellowship, will take forward this debate.

During eighteen years of Conservative government, relations between our party and Britain's churches were at times a little uneasy. I dare say that there were faults and misunderstandings on both sides. Now we have the opportunity to engage in a new and creative dialogue about the future of our country.

No institution can match the long experience of the Christian Church of grappling with social problems and working for the good of mankind, while at the same time always proclaiming that each individual human being is precious in the eyes of God. The Conservative Party is changing in order to regain the trust of the British people, but we shall never change our basic beliefs in freedom, in enterprise, in the family and in strong local institutions. I claim for our party no monopoly of Christian compassion, but I firmly believe that the moral tradition of Wilberforce and Shaftesbury, which runs like a golden thread through the history of the Conservative Party, means that we can take pride in the values and principles for which we stand.

Politicians have to work with the reality of the world as we find it. Our scope for action will always have practical limits; no amount of politics is going to build the Kingdom of God. The Christian Church, both in its faith and its works, has a well of experience and insight from which any sensible politician will wish to draw. I look forward to discussing with Britain's churches in the months and years ahead how we can take forward our common goal of securing the peace and prosperity of the British people. I hope that we can learn from one another.

1999

Charles Moore

With that famous precision of mind which was so unsuited to the compromises of politics, Enoch Powell used to say that nobody was really justified in calling themselves a Christian. It was impossible to know what the word really meant, he claimed. All you could say with any safety, Enoch argued, was that you were a member of a particular church. In that spirit, I speak to you tonight as a member, by conversion, of the Roman Catholic Church, who is also a Conservative; although I hasten to say that I am not a spokesman for that church.

It is very difficult indeed to say what Christianity is, and this fact should make all of us more diffident than we usually are. In such company, I certainly feel diffident tonight. Is there any connection in my mind, then, between being a Catholic – or, in the case of others, an Anglican, a Methodist or whatever – and a Conservative? At the most important level, I would say there is none. Faith is a gift of grace, not a matter of opinion. Political allegiance is merely a matter of opinion, and of habit and prejudice. Faith concerns what is perfectly true: politics is just a question of somehow, imperfectly, getting by.

Many talks to forums such as these devote themselves to seeking to show that Conservatism and Christian belief go well together.

I do not want to attempt that task tonight. I am absolutely convinced that Conservatives can be good Christians, but then I believe exactly the same of socialists. Christians can justifiably support any party that does not explicitly reject the Christian God, as communist parties do and the Nazi Party, slightly less directly, did. There are, or have been, Christians who sincerely believe that a police state, or complete nationalisation, or capital punishment, or 98 per cent income tax, or the feudal system, or slavery, or apartheid, or the confiscation of private property can be made compatible with their religion. I do not think we can say that they are definitely wrong; as long as they refrain from saying they are definitely right. It is tolerable, though silly, to say that you think Jesus would have voted for Margaret Thatcher or Tony Blair. It is intolerable to suggest that Christian belief must go with one political creed – that any political party can be holier than thou.

For the sobering thing about Christianity is how radically critical it is of all politics. There is only one phrase about politics in that document that would now be called the mission statement of Christianity, but which you and I know as the Creed. It is: 'He suffered under Pontius Pilate'. This event was the point in history at which divine power intersected with temporal human power. In temporal, human terms, politics came off better than religion. Jesus was executed and Pontius Pilate remained governor of Judea. But it is an article of our faith that, in terms of the divine plan, politics and the world it represented were overcome, then and forever.

Poor Pilate. I feel some sympathy for him because he reminds me of a slightly cowardly British colonial civil servant in a tight spot. He is the eternal representative of politics in the great drama of the universe. He has authority: he uses it to do the wrong thing and yet he is, fundamentally, powerless. He is not so much Everyman as Every Minister. His only capacity – which, to do him justice, he is reluctant to employ – is to inflict suffering on others. That phrase

'He suffered under Pontius Pilate' is Christianity's epitaph for politics and politicians.

This is not because politicians are seen in Christian tradition as peculiarly wicked people. They are, rather, typically wicked people – types of the human race in its desire for power and status and for everything that almost all of us want but are fundamentally not worth having. (Editors, by the way, are another example of the same type.) Again and again in the New Testament, the valuation that 'the world' puts on things is set at naught. The Gospels encourage us to think that only the poor are truly rich, that the weak are strong, that you should turn the other cheek to your enemy, that you must become as little children to enter the Kingdom of Heaven, that God puts down the mighty from their seat and exalts the humble and meek.

'The world' – that is to say, the way human beings naturally run their own affairs – cannot accept such calls. You couldn't run a society without power and money and a system by which some have more of it than others. Nor, indeed – and this is a point socialists miss – do the Gospels say that you can. What they do say is that such a system is far, very far, from what the service of God requires. When Thatcherites such as myself argue that, for example, the Good Samaritan could not have been much use in rescuing the man who fell among thieves if he had not had any money, we are right, but we are also whistling in the dark to keep our spirits up. That parable, surely, is not about money, but about our absolute obligation towards people to whom 'the world' thinks we have no obligation at all.

I once heard a sermon by a financially prudent church minister – and perhaps it will not surprise you that this was in Scotland – who had solemnly counted all the parables of our Lord and declared that 'no fewer than sixteen' (I think it was) 'concerned hard cash'. I fear the Gospel message about hard cash is less comforting than this gentleman appeared to believe. But lest anyone think this line of argument leads inexorably to socialism, I would challenge all those who make that leap so glibly. How do they know that Christ's injunction to the young man 'to sell all that he hath and give it to the poor' demands punitive taxation? By what right do they arrogate to governments the authority to impose by law a vision of a kingdom which is, in the famous words, 'not of this world'? To choose to sell all that you have is quite a different thing from having it confiscated from you by the state.

No, I am being totally impartial here between left and right, like the BBC. My message is simply that the disjunction between a life in the service of God and a life in the practice of politics is extreme. In my view, it follows from this that the most admirable politicians will be those who handle everything touching religion with humility, and are very hesitant to enlist it in their cause. They should always remember G. K. Chesterton's famous poem of rebuke to F. E. Smith when, absurdly, he called the Welsh Disestablishment Bill 'a bill which has shocked the conscience of every Christian community in Europe':

> For your legal cause or civil
> You fight well and get your fee;
> For your God or dream or devil
> You will answer, not to me.
> Talk about the pews and steeples
> And the cash that goes therewith!
> But the souls of Christian peoples ...
> Chuck it, Smith!

I think it was Disraeli who said that he didn't mind Mr Gladstone having the ace of trumps up his sleeve, but he did object to his suggesting that the Almighty put it there.

Some of you will remember an incident just before this party's conference in the year of the great miners' strike. The then Archbishop of Canterbury, Dr Runcie, had given an interview in which he criticised what he thought was government harshness towards the miners. Lord Whitelaw, at that time, I think, deputy Prime Minister, was interviewed in reply and he said: 'I'd just like to say two things. First, the Archbishop was a very gallant officer in the war. Second, he's a very religious man.' At the time, I thought this was laughable. I reckoned Dr Runcie deserved a good kicking.

But that only shows how much more un-Christian than Willie Whitelaw I am. Even if, as I believe, Dr Runcie was in the wrong, Willie wanted to defer to something which he knew was more important than politics. That was a tactful and dignified thing to do. Well, we have come this far, and I appear to be preaching a comfortless message. I seem to be saying that all politics is irredeemably bad and that no one who wishes to follow Christ should have anything to do with it.

One implication of my words would appear to be that this Conservative Christian Fellowship under whose auspices we meet is a contradiction in terms and should be wound up at once. No, not so. For I think that modern experience teaches that if there is one thing worse than a politics that drags Christianity in, it is a politics that drives Christianity out. Even politicians are representatives of the human race. They speak not only to a brief, but as participants in the continuous conversation of civilisation. If that conversation loses touch with the language and beliefs of Christianity, it becomes harsh and cold and trivial.

We can see this happening with particular clarity today because of an accident of time. The millennium is the year which marks, slightly inaccurately, the 2,000th birthday of Jesus Christ. It has been instructive, and depressing, to see how this occasion is being marked by those who govern us.

Britain has chosen to celebrate the millennium with a dome.

This is said to be the most expensive building ever erected. It is more than twice the size of Wembley Stadium and looks – I see it every day from my office – like a space ship about to disgorge a vast alien population from another planet. As you know, there has been endless wrangling about what should be in the Dome, but the one thing all those involved have agreed it should not be is a celebration or even a commemoration of Jesus Christ. Grudgingly, they have permitted some sort of representation of something or other to do with religion, known as the 'Faith Zone'.

Even more grudgingly, and only, apparently, after the intervention of the Queen, have they permitted the Archbishop of Canterbury to say a short prayer on New Year's Eve. And they have insisted that this take place at 11.15 p.m., so as not to spoil anybody's fun at the great moment of midnight. This is, or should be, a birthday party, but what children call the Birthday King will not be enthroned. The absence of Jesus is eloquent of the real concerns of those who lead us today. There will be celebrations of commerce and of media, of companies such as BT, BSkyB, British Airways and Boots. There will be rock stars and TV stars and fireworks and there will be Tony Blair. It's not far short of the Tower of Babel. And so a chance that comes only once in a thousand years will have been missed.

One reason advanced by the authorities for this refusal to recognise that the millennium is a Christian occasion is that this might offend other faiths. In fact, this is conspicuously untrue. Muslim leaders in Britain, whose faith, of course, recognises Jesus as a great prophet, have supported the idea of a Christian-led celebration. So, eloquently, has the Chief Rabbi, Dr Jonathan Sacks. Men of faith nowadays have small difficulty in looking for the important things that unite them with other religions and encouraging one another. Nor is it the case, as one is often told, that there is no public appetite for the study of Christianity or the life and teaching and legacy of Jesus.

I have a small, recent experience of this. At the *Daily Telegraph* a few months ago, we launched, with some trepidation, a six-part magazine series called *AD*, which was a history of Christianity from its beginnings to the present day. Even I, who had thought up the project, had been by no means certain that it would be a commercial success. In the event, we sold 25,000 extra copies every day that we published, sold out of binders to keep the series in and now, by popular demand, have brought it out in book form. This Saturday, we shall launch a free gift of the Four Gospels in the paper. People actually are hungry for such things, aware of a gap in their lives and in our culture.

Contemplating the spectacle of the Dome, one realises that 'dumbing down' is not a phrase solely to describe daytime television and the softer features purveyed in my own trade in Fleet Street. It goes to the very top. Perhaps we should call it 'Doming down'. It describes the way we are led, the whole character of our politics. Thinking of the emptiness of the Millennium Dome, the Bishop of London has declared that he wants to advertise his own cathedral – St Paul's – with the slogan 'the Dome that knows what's inside it'.

There is a similar problem of emptiness and evacuation and lack of faith in too many of our institutions. Why does Chris Patten feel that it can be good for the policing of part of the United Kingdom to remove the symbols of that kingdom, such as the crown and the picture of the Queen, from the RUC? Why do MPs queue up for humiliatingly short appearances on television instead of debating the making of laws in the House of Commons? What is it, to use Shakespeare's phrase, that has 'stolen hence the life of the building'?

I would argue that part of the explanation is that we really are, at last, becoming a post-Christian society. Although church attendance has been low for a very long time, it is only in the last thirty years that most people have been brought up knowing practically nothing whatever about the faith that has shaped their culture, informed their language, given most of them their name and built a bond between them and other Christian countries. At my village primary school in the mid-sixties, it was assumed without question that we would all study the Bible, reading the Authorised Version, and that we would learn by heart many of the collects from the Book of Common Prayer. And because it was assumed, it worked. There can't be a school in the state sector where that is true today.

The early generations of those who rejected Christianity retained many of its characteristics. The legacy of Protestantism gave them a reverence for the written word and for personal honesty and moral seriousness. That of Catholicism gave them a belief in community and in the blessings of poverty, and left vestiges of a sacramental attitude towards creation. As the Christian experience becomes more distant, though, all this decays. The decline of the quality of what is taught in schools is directly related to the loss of the belief that a particular text is sacred. If you discard the idea of the Good Book, you more gradually discard the idea of good books in general and end up with the idea that there is no real difference between good and bad books. The criterion of value goes.

When this happens, the need that religion supplies does not, of course, disappear. It simply gets ministered to in worse ways. The reaction to the death of the Princess of Wales two years ago showed a society in the grip of feelings which religious faith would have done so much to direct and satisfy. The need to blame would have been balanced by the need to forgive. The need to mourn would have been balanced by the need to give thanks. The urge to worship became for some a sort of idolatry. There was an atmosphere of superstition and hysteria typical of the religious impulse when it is separated from all rules. I thought it was interesting and encouraging that what brought a divided nation together after an extremely difficult week was a funeral service which combined a modern approachability with a more or less orthodox Anglican form. The liturgy helped to heal.

Our politicians play a part in this post-Christian drama. Some of them, individually serious Christians, evoke in a ghostly or, occasionally ghastly way the language of belief. Was I being over-interpretative when I detected in Mr Blair's words two years ago, 'one cross on the ballot paper, one nation reborn', a tasteless suggestion that Britain had been crucified under the Conservatives and resurrected under Labour? I don't know, but I do know that New Labour exploits the appeal of religion while studiously avoiding its content. It is somehow typical, I think, that Mr Blair was discovered to have been regularly taking Roman Catholic communion while avoiding actually becoming a Catholic. He was, as it were, claiming club privilege without paying the membership fee.

One of the key tests of a Christian is witness. Indeed, the original meaning of the word 'martyr' is witness. One of the tests of witness is whether your Christianity leads you to do something to your personal disadvantage because of what you believe. How does Tony Blair look against that test? He says he is against abortion, but he votes for it. He sends his children to a traditional Catholic school, but when the headmaster, deprived of grant by Labour's educational reforms, asks parents to contribute money, our Prime Minister's press secretary is authorised to brief against the man and say how lucky he is that Mr Blair has made him famous. Speaking as a journalist, I have never seen a British government so constructed around black propaganda and lies. I don't expect our Prime Ministers to be saints – indeed, it annoys me that Mr Blair never travels without his halo – but I do expect them not to let untruth be their chief currency of communication. So the more Mr Blair talks of his moral crusade the quicker I start counting the spoons.

No, we cannot look to our leaders – not even to the redoubtable Ann Widdecombe – to Christianise our politics. Like early Christians in a hostile environment, we surely have to go back to the core of our faith as it relates to the world in which we live. To do this we must concentrate again on the Incarnation. The fact that God took on human flesh, actually became a man, is the most explosive and distinctive aspect of Christianity.

In the nineteenth century, the force of this doctrine led many to become Christian socialists. They wanted to see Christ's love translated into the actions of the state and visible in the condition of the poor. We today may think them naive, but we must recognise that they were asking the right questions. Today, the challenge of how to bring out the Christ-like dignity of each human being takes new forms. In the West, at least, we are no longer so beset with problems of hungry mouths and premature deaths and disgraceful housing. Jesus's claim that the poor are always with us has become, in purely economic terms, very nearly untrue. Instead, human dignity is assaulted by different threats. I will select three and leave it at that.

The first is the growing notion that there is no moral difference between human beings and animals. This sounds like a kind view, leading to good treatment for animals. In fact, it leads to a denial of our duty of stewardship, and a persecution of good people whose living involves the rearing, training or killing of animals. It is not a coincidence that Jesus lived on earth as a man rather than a hedgehog or an elephant. Mankind has a unique responsibility, and the more we deny this the crueller we will become to one another. Nor is it a coincidence that those who wax most sentimental about animals often have an anti-Christian contempt for people. Hitler abolished fox-hunting at much the same time as he began systematic persecution of the Jews.

The second threat is the perversion of science. Wonderful advances in knowledge, good in themselves, have led some people to believe that human identity is a meaningless concept. I notice that misinterpretation of discoveries about genes is leading people to say that no human being is anything more than a particular programming of a genetic code. They say that moral choice is therefore meaningless and that it is the job of society to 'produce' –

they always like the mechanical language of production – to produce people suitable for its wants. People with the wrong shape or colour or sex or brain or other genetic predisposition would be screened out of our species, in the supposed interest of the rest of us. Christians in the twentieth century are used to standing up for the preservation of human life. In the twenty-first century, they will have to fight for its very definition.

Finally, I turn to what is known as political correctness. Much of this creed presses Christian phrases into service and is supported by some sincere Christians. Justified hatred of the oppression of black people or of women has led some to support anything that appears to advance their cause. Their good motives should be respected.

But the truth about political correctness is very different. It is part of the totalitarian campaign, which, having lost the battle of economics, has opened up another front. In the old days, socialists wanted to nationalise the means of production. Today, they want to nationalise people. Indeed, given what I said earlier about the march of science, they see people as the key means of production. Politically correct politicians – and they dominate the Labour Party – want to control the way people are: what thoughts they have about race and sex and class and nation, how they bring up their children. They want a sixteen-year-old boy to be free to have sex with a forty-year-old man but to be punished for smoking. They want fox hunters to go to prison but IRA terrorist murderers to go free. They speak a great deal of 'human rights', but they approve only of certain categories of human being.

And so when I heard Tony Blair tell his conference last week that in the eighteenth century our main resource was land, in the nineteenth century and twentieth century it was plant and capital, but that today it is people, I'm afraid I did not rejoice. People are not a 'resource' for politicians. They are the race in whom God took shape on earth, and each person is unique.

Mr Blair said last week that his party offered 'the nation's only hope of salvation'. The only hope? As we approach the 2,000th anniversary of the moment when our salvation came down among us, we are justified in echoing G. K. Chesterton and saying 'Chuck it! Blair'. As individuals, Conservatives are no better and no worse than socialists. But our political beliefs do at least make it harder for us to sustain a complete arrogance about our role in the life of our nation. So here is a good task for an opposition party. Let us put down the mighty from their seat, and magnify the Lord at the same time.

Brian Griffiths

William Wilberforce stands out in British history as one of the great social reformers of the nineteenth century. Although he is associated in the public mind with the campaigns to abolish the transatlantic slave trade and then slavery itself, he took up many other causes, such as penal reform, medical aid for the poor, education for the deaf, restrictions on the use of child labour, an improvement in the conditions of the Poor Law and the reform of morals.

At the age of twenty-six he experienced a religious conversion which influenced his life and thinking, and especially his approach to politics. From that time on his life was taken up with a commitment to remedy injustice, to help the poor and to strengthen moral standards. He was a member of the House of Commons for nearly fifty years, though he stood as an independent and not as a Tory because he believed that the concept of party was divisive. Despite his rejection of a party label he was a close friend and supporter of the Prime Minister William Pitt, and his views on most political issues would have put him firmly in the camp of someone whom today we would call a Conservative.

The title I have chosen for this Address is 'Conservatism and Christianity'. It is an ambitious subject and at the risk of stating the obvious it is necessary to make certain points clear at the outset.

One is that we should never lose sight of the contrasting nature of religion and politics. The Christian religion is an account of eternal truth. It is an explanation of our origin and our destiny. It is about the purposes of God and the salvation of mankind. The book of Genesis starts with the ringing declaration 'In the beginning God created the heavens and the earth', while the Revelation of John is a vision of a new heaven and a new earth, a final judgment and an eternity of torment. The Incarnation is the story of how God took human form and died on a cross for the redemption of mankind with the result that the Christian faith is an answer to the most searching questions we can ever ask of ourselves. Who am I? What is the purpose of life? Can I know God? Is there life after death?

By contrast politics deals with something of a totally different character, namely the activity of governing in this world. It is an activity that is specific and limited. It is concerned with the temporal, the things of Caesar, not the spiritual, the things of God. It is about expediency and the art of the possible. As a result no political doctrine, creed, ideology or even disposition should ever claim an exclusive status because it is in some way based uniquely on the Christian religion. Conservatism has no monopoly of Christian understanding. I believe that the Christian faith has relevance to politics, but this relationship is neither simple nor direct. We cannot extract unambiguous statements from the Bible that will give detailed guidance on proposed legislation. At every stage in dealing with a political issue, namely defining the problem, devising a policy and then drafting legislation, and even with regard to issues such as abortion, divorce and homosexuality, which some might think are very straightforward, there will be many detailed practical considerations which will of necessity have to be taken into account, not least because a law which is put on the statute book must be something that is enforceable.

Although religion and politics are essentially different kinds of activities – a point made so eloquently in St Augustine's *The City of God* – the Christian must wary of dualism. To say that they are different is not to say that they bear no relationship to each other. The Christian faith provides a framework for understanding the created world and therefore the setting in which government must exist.

A second point that needs to be made is that the Conservative party has never been, or aspired to be, a Christian party. In this respect the Conservative Party is different from the Christian democratic parties that exist in many countries in continental Europe. It has never been based on a religious credo. It has always been open to people of all faiths and to people of no faith. It has accommodated within its ranks people committed to very different lifestyles. Certain of its leaders have been people of faith, even deep faith, but this has typically been expressed in personal terms and not publicly paraded as a party credential. In fact the exact opposite has been the case. Conservative politicians have taken to heart Burke's words that 'politics and the pulpit are terms that have little agreement', with the result that they tend to be careful, even to a fault, in ensuring that they can never be open to the charge that they have used religion to secure votes.

Having said this, it is also the case that since the title 'Conservative' was used as a party label in the early nineteenth century, the argument for Conservatism, beginning with Edmund Burke, has been based on a religious world view and, in particular, on the truth of the Christian religion. There have been exceptions, perhaps the most notable being Michael Oakeshott, but in general the case for Conservatism has been presented as inextricably linked to religion. That is certainly the conclusion of F. J. Hearnshaw's study *Conservatism in England*, published in the 1930s, and of Russell Kirk's scholarly work *The Conservative Mind*, published in the early 1950s. It might be thought that Anthony Quinton's study *The Politics of Imperfection*, which is an attempt to detach Conservatism from its religious roots, leads to the opposite conclusion. He argues that there have been agnostics who have argued the case for Conservatism, just as much as Christians; that in the writings of Burke, Newman and Salisbury, their religious beliefs are not crucial to their political views, and that what all Conservatives have in common is a view of the imperfection of mankind, which can be deduced from other than religious principles. Of these three points, the first is certainly true, though the only example he provides since Burke is Oakeshott, whose Conservatism is limited by his secular assumptions, the second I would strongly dispute; and the third, while correct as far as it goes, is a rather limited conception of Conservatism. Let me give some examples.

One of the most important catalysts leading to the formation of the Conservative Party was the French Revolution. Burke said of the French Revolution that it was 'the most astonishing crisis that has hitherto happened in the world'. It was something radical, experimental, bloody, chaotic, a 'monstrous tragic-comic scene' in which property was confiscated, the Church was plundered, family and traditions were undermined, the monarchy was overthrown and irreligion encouraged. In his *Reflections on the Revolution in France*, published in 1790, Burke attacked the revolutionaries and their sympathisers in this country, but invariably with arguments that were firmly rooted in the religious nature of man and the religious basis of society. 'We know, and it is our pride to know', he asserts, 'that man is by his constitution a religious animal: that atheism is against, not only our reason but our instincts; and that it cannot prevail long', from which it followed that 'religion is the basis of civil society and the source of all good and of all comfort', and in particular that 'the Christian religion has hitherto been our boost and comfort, and one great source of civilisation amongst us'. It would not be too strong to say that virtually every statement of a Conservative approach to politics since the time of Burke has acknowledged its debt to the *Reflections*.

Certainly Burke's sentiments were echoed by Disraeli: 'The most powerful principle which governs man is the religious principle . . . A wise government, allying itself with religion, would as it were consecrate society, and sanctify the state.' Or again:

> The spiritual nature of man is stronger than codes or constitutions. No government can endure which does not recognise that for its foundation and no legislation last which does not flow from that fountain. The principle may develop itself in manifold forms, in the shape of many creeds and many churches. But the principle is divine. As time is divided into day and night, so religion rests upon the Providence of God and the responsibility of man.

At first sight John Henry Newman may be an unlikely candidate to be thought of as a conservative philosopher: he was ordained in the Church of England at the age of twenty-three, was one of the leaders of the Oxford Movement, became a cardinal in the Roman Catholic Church and wrote no treatise on political philosophy. But in a series of articles in *The Times* in 1841, he made a stinging attack on Robert Peel's Tamworth Manifesto, and said in later life: 'I have no great love for the Conservatives.' Yet Russell Kirk and Anthony Quinton both conclude that Newman, although not in any sense a politician, was the master of philosophical conservatism in the Victorian era.

He was a conservative with a small 'c'. His conservatism was founded on his religious beliefs, and in particular the emphasis which he placed on the significance of the fall of mankind and the doctrine of original sin, allied to a belief in the order and harmony of the visible world, which mirrored the reality of the invisible world, and reflected the providence of God, and of which the state and every individual is a part.

His conservatism showed itself in many ways. He was a relentless opponent of liberalism. He had a profound sense of the law and order that existed in the world – not simply of the laws at work in the physical universe but also the existence of laws in the moral, political and social spheres as well. He attached great importance to the wisdom embodied in institutions 'which have stood the trial and received the sanction of ages' and which as a consequence do not depend on the vagaries of individuals. He placed great value on tradition, which to him was more than the ideas embodied in institutions or the handing down of intellectual traditions. It was something unwritten, certainly, but best expressed in the way society has felt or behaved during a period of time and something that, he claimed, could not therefore be conveyed easily in a set of propositions.

Similarly the two great statements of Conservatism in the twentieth century, *Conservatism* by Lord Hugh Cecil, published in 1912, and *The Case for Conservatism* by Quintin Hogg, published in 1959, make the Christian faith central to their defence of Conservatism.

In his book, which is probably the finest statement ever made of a Conservative position, Lord Hugh Cecil argues that in any discussion of political principles we must have some standards of right and wrong to which they conform, and he is very clear in basing his on those in the New Testament. He is unable, therefore, to discuss issues such as the claims of rich and poor, the operations of a competitive market economy, the problem of poverty, measures for ameliorating the condition of the people, and the content and structure of national education, without reference to religion. He considered it a scandal to Christianity that large numbers of people in the country lived in poverty and misery, and was firmly of the view that Christianity stood for social reform. 'To the Conservative this purpose comes with a sacred sanction, for the religious foundation of his Tory beliefs gives to the sorrows of the poor an urgent claim upon his care.' More than that he emphasised that religion was not only directly relevant to political issues, but had an indirect influence, because any political matter that raised issues of moral obligation could not be addressed without reference to Christian standards. One of the fascinating parts of the chapter in his book that deals with religion and politics is the ethics of a competitive market economy.

His conclusion was that

> the championship of religion is the most important of the functions of Conservatism. It is the keystone of the arch upon which the whole fabric rests. As long as Conservatism makes the fulfilment of its duties to religion the first of its purposes, it will be saved from the two principal dangers that alternatively threaten it: the danger of sinking into a mere factious variation of Liberalism, supporting the claims of another set of politicians, but propounding measures not distinguished by any pervading principle, or the other danger of standing only for the defence of those who are well off, without any sincere endeavour to consider the interests of the whole people, or any higher object than the triumph of the sagacious selfishness of the prosperous. Religion is the standard by which the plans of politicians must be judged, and a religious purpose must purify their aims and methods. Emphasising this truth, Conservatism will be the creed neither of a superfluous faction nor of a selfish class.

In terms of the Conservative Party he said: 'Conservatism must not shrink from the appeal to Christian morality. Its characteristic as a party ought to be, in view of its past as its future, the readiness to apply a religious standard to politics.'

In *The Case for Conservatism*, Quintin Hogg, now Lord Hailsham, says that he 'pondered desperately long' before writing the chapter in his book which deals with religion and society. It is the opening chapter of a section which deals with basic Conservative ideas, and is placed at the beginning of the section because it logically precedes those ideas which we traditionally associate with Conservatism, such as the organic nature of society, political liberty, private property, the rule of law, individual enterprise and continuity as a condition of progress, and the wisdom embodied in traditions and institutions. Hailsham says that he despised nothing more than a politician who used religion to advance his politics – 'the end of honest politics' he termed it – but he went on to say: 'Nevertheless, I am compelled to write what I believe to be true, and I am fortified in my belief by the fact that I can discover no important writer on Conservatism who has not been driven to the same conclusion', namely that 'there can be no genuine Conservatism which is not founded upon a religious view of the basis of civil obligation, and there can be no true religion where the basis of civil obligation is treated as purely secular'. He says that he was driven to this conclusion because he found that he could not divorce his political faith from his ultimate view of reality.

Although he is most recognised for his contribution to literature, the notion that religion should underpin the political philosophy of conservatism with a small 'c' comes out very clearly from certain of the writings of T. S. Eliot. A political philosophy, he suggests, is not simply a set of policies or programmes for a political party, but a way of life for a people. For a political philosophy to grasp this it must reach down to what he calls 'the substratum of collective temperament', to 'ways of behaviour and unconscious values'. In fact he was explicit in recognising that this would lead to the religious roots of society. 'As political philosophy derives its sanction from ethics, and ethics from the truth of religion, it is only by returning to the eternal source of truth that we can hope for any social organisation which will not, to its ultimate destruction, ignore some essential aspect of reality.'

He published *The Idea of a Christian Society* in 1939 against the background of the growth of fascism in Europe. If a small number of people could have such a devastating and evil impact in their countries, could not a small number of Christians have an influence for good?

In the book he posed the choice facing society at that time in stark terms, namely to advance further in the direction of a pagan society, with its materialistic and stunted culture, or to choose a religiously based society that, however imperfect, would be vastly superior to the liberal alternative. Despite the sanctity which had been attached to the word in the Western world, he was scathing in his attack on liberalism because he argued it would destroy the social habits of the people, dissolve their natural collective consciousness into individual constituents, license the opinions of the most foolish by replacing education with instruction, encourage cleverness rather than wisdom, and the upstart rather than the qualified. Liberalism was defined more by its starting point as a movement away from something, rather than by the end which it would bring. It was something that released energy rather than conserving it. His concern was that its end might be very different from that which it intended, a sort of nihilistic chaos which would require as a remedy some form of brutalised control.

But in contrast to liberalism he also attacked Conservatism with a capital 'C'. This was not necessarily a philosophy of life, and indeed may be no more than a set of habits, with the result that it was not something which could guide us. Because of this it was just as repellent as liberalism and would result in 'petrifaction'. It could not, he claimed, within its own limits of simply being a conservative disposition, answer the question 'What must be preserved?'

This could only be done, he suggested many years later in an address called 'The Literature of Politics', which he gave to the Conservative Political Centre, by reaching down into what he called the pre-political. It recalls his earlier emphasis on political philosophy and he characterised it as 'the stratum down to which any sound political thinking must push its roots, and from which it must derive its nourishment. It is also, if you don't mind my changing the metaphor so abruptly, the land in which dwell the Gods of the Copy

Book Headings; and, abandoning figurative language altogether, it is the domain of ethics, in the end, the domain of theology. For the question of questions, which no political philosophy can escape, and by the right answer to which all political thinking must in the end be judged, is simply this: What is Man? What are his limitations? What is his misery and what his greatness? And what, finally, is his destiny?'

It is to this question of questions posed by Eliot that we must now turn; because it is in answer to this that we are able to understand why Conservatism has been built on a religious foundation.

In the first place Christianity provides an answer to Eliot's question, and in answering it shows why society needs a religious basis. The point of departure for the Christian is that we live in a world God created, not in a universe that is the product of chance. We are part of his creation. As the Hebrew text puts it, we have been made in his image; we possess a mind, a soul, a will, a conscience. We are capable of anger and of love. It is to him we are accountable and answerable. We are restless, homeless, lost, ultimately unfulfilled independently of God. He is the source of all truth. For Edmund Burke to say, therefore, that man is by his constitution a religious animal is to accept the authority of God and to reject the autonomy of man. It is to acknowledge our dependence on divine providence. It is to realise our place in the order of the universe. It is to admit the truth of moral laws, which set out the meaning of right and wrong, and which make social life possible; laws which we could no more invent than we could the physical laws of the universe.

Perhaps the implication of this view can be seen by comparing John Maynard Keynes's description of life in the Bloomsbury Group with Edmund Burke's understanding of obligation in human society. Keynes said of his friends and himself:

> We repudiated entirely customary morals, conventions and traditional wisdom. We were, that is to say, in the strict sense of the term,

immoralists. The consequences of being found out had, of course, to be considered for what they were worth. But we recognised no moral obligation on us, no inner sanction, to conform or to obey. Before heaven we came to be our own judge in our own case.

Contrast this with Burke in his *Reflections*:

We fear God; we look up with awe to kings; with affection to parliaments; with duty to magistrates; with reverence to priests; and with respect to nobility. Why? Because when such ideas are brought before our minds it is to be affected; because all other feelings are fake and spurious, and tend to corrupt our minds, to vitiate our primary morals, to render us unfit for rational liberty; and by teaching us a servile, licentious and abandoned insolence, to be our low sport for a few holidays, to make us perfectly fit for, and justly deserving of slavery, through the whole course of our lives.

To declare that religion is the basis of civil society is to recognise first and foremost that society can only function effectively when we accept moral obligations and acknowledge personal responsibility. This is true of life within a family, a school, a company, indeed within any human institution, including the state. These obligations could, in principle, be based on any set of ethics, including of course those which make no appeal to religion. But the contrast between those based on a secular liberal ethic and those based on a revealed religion is important. In the case of Judaism, the injunctions 'Thou shalt' and 'Thou shalt not' were written down on tablets of stone. They were unambiguous and they carried sanctions. The reason the attempt to construct morality on a secular basis is so uncertain and unreliable is precisely because of its lack of absolutes and its absence of sanctions.

A society that accepts religion as its basis will be one in which obligations entered into by individuals are reflected in the constitution and practices of its institutions, monarchy, parliament, government, church, family and schools. Each will claim a moral legitimacy based on an obligation to God. It is because of our religious heritage that we have the coronation oath, the prayers said at the beginning of each daily session of Parliament, the established church, the special nature of the marriage contract, the significance attached to private property, the distinctive character of church schools and the fiscal incentives that have traditionally been given to charitable institutions. A Conservative will value these as part of our tradition, but it is important to notice that it is a tradition embodying truths and virtues which have as their source the Christian religion. Newman, who placed great emphasis on the importance of tradition as an initial way of understanding, makes the same point when he recognises that in the end tradition requires 'some ultimate authority to make it trustworthy'. I do not believe this is a statement that could have been made by Michael Oakeshott.

In history we have seen many attempts to construct civil society without a religious basis: the French Revolution, Nazi Germany and atheistic Marxism in the Soviet Union, eastern Europe and parts of Asia come readily to mind. The consequences of such attempts are instructive for two reasons. First, although they sought to eradicate traditional religion, they created in reality an alternative ideology which turned out to be just as 'religious' as the religion they sought to discard. Second, the violence, disruption, uncertainty, fear and human suffering created in these instances points to the weakness of political experiments based on nothing but theory and ideology. These, of course, are not the choices we face today, but there is a powerful tendency to establish a purely secular society detached from its Christian roots in which the unifying principle is nothing more than a hedonistic libertarianism based on the slogan 'freedom of choice', and for which we have no historical precedent that it will ever be successful.

One insight of the Christian religion that has been particularly emphasised by Conservatives is the moral and intellectual imperfection of human nature. The doctrine of original sin is perhaps the least popular and the most offensive of all Christian teaching, and yet, ironically, the one for which there is such overwhelming evidence. Far from human nature being naturally good and pure, inclined to act virtuously, Wilberforce reckoned that the language of Christianity was humiliating.

'From it', he says, 'we learn that man is an apostate creature, fallen from his high original, degraded in his nature, deprived in his faculties, prone to vice, disinclined to virtue; he is tainted with sin not slightly and superficially, but radically and to the very core.' He pronounces man as majestic yet in ruin. The dignity of man is that he has been created a child of God; the tragedy of man is that he has chosen a life of total self-centredness.

I believe that Wilberforce's interpretation of Christian teaching is correct, but one misunderstanding should be avoided. The fact of the inherent depravity of human nature does not mean that every act of every individual is sinful. The image of God in man may be defaced but it remains recognisable. People without faith can demonstrate remarkable acts of charity, altruism and sacrifice. The fall of man is total in that every facet of his being is affected, but that does not mean that he has been reduced to a brute. Curiously enough, it is those who attempt to live by the highest standards, such as the mystics, who have known most and described so convincingly the extent of this self-centredness.

How does this relate to Conservatism? Conservatism is built on scepticism of change, partly because of a distrust of the unknown and partly because of a regard for the familiar. The familiar is something that has been tried, is known to work, has been handed on, typically personally, and has been taught by example. By the same token history teaches us to be guarded about political experiments, untested programmes, or some leap in the dark, especially when it is associated with some new theory or ideology. The doctrine of original sin is a powerful basis for caution in the face of utopian rhetoric. It is the reason we can be sure that the Kingdom of God will not be built through revolution, legislation or the decrees of government. We have, in this life, as a result, to settle for something far less romantic and idealistic. As a consequence of this the Conservative will be realistic about what government can achieve and aim not for the ideal but for the possible.

Such pessimism over the potential of fallen human nature, however, should not be an obstacle to reform. Indeed the very opposite should be the case. 'A state without the means of some change is without the means of its conservation,' remarked Burke. Reforms which are properly thought out, which redress obvious grievances, and which are acceptable to the electorate, are both necessary and desirable.

Another emphasis of Christian theology is the significance it attaches to liberty. In the history of the Jews, the feast of the Passover is the celebration of their freedom from slavery in Egypt. Israel could not become the society God intended while it suffered the indignities of slavery. Political liberty gave the Jewish people the freedom to worship and build an economic and social order that would embody the ideals of their faith. That faith saw every person as being of infinite worth, possessed of dignity, because they had been created in the image of God. A respect for the dignity of the individual person is the primary focus of Christian ethics, so that the protection of individual liberty and property has been characteristically a legitimate Christian concern.

Conservatism has recognised the importance of liberty by ensuring that the constitution maintains a balance between authority and freedom, and protects individuals and their property, material and immaterial, against injustice through the rule of law. The major threat to individual liberty has come from the state, which accounts for the emphasis placed especially on economic freedom by post-war governments in Britain. The Judeo-Christian defence of liberty is, however, radically different from the idea of freedom embraced by the philosophers of the Enlightenment, which took as its starting point the autonomy of man. The Christian defence of freedom is not of unlimited freedom, but of freedom within a moral order in which there are well-defined limits.

A fourth theme that I would like to extract from Christian theology which is of extreme importance to this subject is the idea of community. The Christian has a distinct conception of God. Christianity is a theistic not a deistic religion, because of the belief that God has entered into a personal relationship with those he created. In addition Christianity is a trinitarian and not a unitarian religion; the Godhead itself is made up of a community of three persons – Father, Son and Holy Spirit – rather than being a solitary, lonely individual extending from eternity to eternity. The theistic and trinitarian basis of Christian theology means that great significance is attached to the notion of community in the created order. Hence the emphasis on the family, the tribe, the village, the city, the church and the nation, each as a separate community through which people establish their identity and live their lives. This theology leads naturally to an organic, rather than an individualistic, view of society. The emphasis is on society as a unitary living entity rather than a collection of individuals held together by law.

Conservatives have always singled out communities, the 'little platoons' as Burke called them which make up civil society, as being of importance. Hence the significance that Conservatives attach today to the need to strengthen civil society. The family, even when under assault from our culture and facing fiscal disincentives, still remains the basic unit of society. In it children are shown love and respect and taught the basic rules of civilised behaviour. They learn the virtues necessary for the development of character. Our children are the future of our society and consequently they deserve special protection from the state. Moreover, a commitment to marriage and stable family life remains the ideal to which most people aspire in society. The family is only one community. Alongside it there are the many others, such as the neighbourhood, the village, the school, corporations, clubs, charities and churches, to which people belong, to which they devote a great deal of time and through which they can work and serve others. Finally there is the nation itself, which is also a distinct community and which has the responsibility not just to defend itself, but to play a responsible part in its relations with others.

Within a Conservative approach it is absolutely essential that these various communities should each be allowed to retain their own integrity and pursue their own objectives, independent of the interfering arm of the state.

A final theme that emerges from the Christian faith is the injunction to love and serve others, especially the poor, and to stand against injustice. Jesus summed up the ten commandments of the Mosaic Law in two statements: to love God with heart, mind, soul and strength and to love our neighbour as ourself. Wilberforce remarked that this grace was 'the indispensable . . . the characteristic duty of Christians'. He argued in the most moving section of his book *A Practical View* that it was cultivated with greatest advantage by meditating on the crucifixion.

> Our hearts become tender while we contemplate this single act of loving kindness. We grow desirous of imitating what we cannot but admire. A vigorous principle of enlarged and active charity springs up within us; and we go forth with alacrity, desirous of treading in the steps of our blessed Master, and of manifesting our gratitude for his unmerited goodness, by bearing each others' burdens, and abounding in the disinterested labours of benevolence.

It may be argued that there is nothing distinctly Conservative in a statement such as this. It is not about tradition, it is not about scepticism, it is not about the wisdom of collective institutions, it is not about the many sources of authority, it is not about continuity. Such a charge is absolutely justified. Such a statement could be made by a liberal, a socialist, a nationalist or a green. But it is important that such a statement not only can, but should and must, be made by Conservatives who profess a Christian faith. The enlarged and active charity, and the disinterested labours of benevolence, of which Wilberforce speaks, are the only response worthy of any Christian, of whatever political persuasion, to the passion and death of Christ.

Those who subscribed to a Conservative political philosophy that has had deep roots in a religious worldview also identified the enemy: it was liberalism. I recognise that Friedrich Hayek has made much of the distinction between continental European liberals, such as the French philosophers from Voltaire to Condorcet, whom he described as constructivist rationalists with their faith in the power of an absolute state to design a structure of centralised government, and those of the Anglo-Scottish Enlightenment such as Bernard Mandeville, David Hume, Adam Ferguson and to a lesser extent Adam Smith, who were the heirs to a more liberal intellectual tradition that recognised the significance of spontaneous forms of adjustment in the social order, and who as a result tended to be non-interventionist, especially in economic affairs. For his purpose, which was to make the case for a free society, this was a valid distinction to make; but from a Christian perspective it is not a helpful one.

Both these groups were unreservedly secular in their thinking. Even though many liberals have recognised the value of religion as a unifying and stabilising force in society, the fact is that they see no inherent reason for a sacred canopy over society. As this is not a created world, individuals are autonomous beings, so that the state has no right to restrict the freedom of individuals, providing they do not harm others. Hayek made it very clear that morals had evolved in an impersonal natural way and he was especially dismissive of those who believed that ethical rules were immutable and eternal. As there is no revealed morality, each individual is free to choose the standards by which they live and the only authority ultimately is the appeal to the reason and judgement of the individual. One may value the wisdom embodied in tradition but in the final analysis Hayek, Mandeville and Hume are as secular in their thinking as any of the continental philosophers from who they wish to distance themselves.

Within this view the idea of original sin is an alien concept: human nature is essentially 'good', or at worse neutral but corrupted by institutions – from one point of view through the inequalities and injustices of capitalism and from another by the unnecessary intervention of the state. Liberals such as these are people of great faith: in their ability to solve social problems by a combination of 'facts' and reason, but certainly without any appeal to 'values'; or through the power of the spontaneous, evolutionary and self-regulating forces of society and the market to produce laws, conventions, morals, language and technical knowledge, which will result in harmony and prosperity.

Liberalism, conceived of as a secular worldview, is still a powerful influence in the political, economic and social fields. In the political field perhaps the most dramatic contemporary example of the kind of liberalism that Conservatism has stood up against is the attempt by the European Union to construct a brand new European super-state, with a commission, a council of ministers, a parliament, a court of justice, a single currency, a single value added tax, a common agricultural policy, a common trading policy, an army, a judiciary, a bureaucracy, a common citizenship, a presidency, a flag, an anthem, as well as the three Maastricht pillars of common monetary, defence and foreign policies, and then to protect the freedom of individuals in law by enunciating a charter of rights. The project is proceeding at a breathtaking pace, and while it lacks the bloodshed and violence of the French Revolution, its grand design starts from the same tabula rasa as the revolutionaries', and pays scant attention to tradition, continuity or legitimacy.

Moreover, the heart of the project is deeply secular. One example of this was the publication, earlier this year, of a new European Union employment directive which sought to strengthen the fight against discrimination at work by extending the traditional grounds on which discrimination is based, namely sex, race and disability, to include religion or belief, age and sexual orientation. In giving evidence to the House of Lords select committee, the senior civil servant from Brussels made it very clear that the intention of the directive was to restrict the ground on which organisations, including religious organisations, could claim exemption from the new proposals. If the directive were to be implemented then, for example, while a religious school could appoint someone of that religion to teach religious instruction in the school, it could not restrict other jobs, such as the teaching of literature, history or health to people of that faith. The UK government along with others fought against the proposed directive, so that safeguards have now been built into the legislation to protect religious schools. Such protection, however, does not extend to partnerships or companies that have been set up on the basis of a religious culture, or to religious charities and religiously based think tanks and lobbying groups. In my judgement only a thoroughgoing secularism could have inspired such a contentious proposal as this.

Liberalism is also a powerful influence in the economic field. Conservatism in Britain today is closely identified with the market economy. Yet a Conservative defence of the market needs to be distanced from that form of secular liberalism which underpins the defence of free markets by economists such as Friedman, Becker and most of all Hayek. The free market is one example of what Hayek describes as a spontaneous social order, namely a self-maintaining or self-regulating system. It allows each individual to pursue their own course of action, while ensuring that at the same time and through some form of competitive mechanism, the whole process leads to continued growth and prosperity. Because of its ability to harness information, a market economy based on private property will systematically outperform any system based on state ownership and state planning. No planning system will ever be able to cope with handling information in this way. Hayek recognises, however, that such a system depends for its existence on the maintenance of certain ethics and values. Typically these have been bourgeois values such as hard work, honesty, restraint, deferred gratification, respect for authority, an obligation to the community and so on. But in the Hayekian scheme these too are the product of cultural evolution, and should not be considered immutable or eternal.

This view of the market economy raises a number of issues; it raises technical issues, such as competition, externalities and various potential inefficiencies, which I think can be dealt with; it raises issues of justice, which I find more difficult, largely because of its insistence that it can say little with respect to distributive justice and the problem of poverty. But most importantly it raises the question of the source of those values which are essential if the market economy is to function. A secular liberal society has no guarantee that it can generate those values that are the necessary basis of a market society. While I believe the evidence shows conclusively that the market economy systematically outperforms any other system of wealth creation, there is at the heart of Hayek's philosophy a fundamental weakness that can only be addressed by a belief in values for which, independently of religion, he has no source.

Perhaps the most topical, and certainly the most tendentious, area of contemporary secular liberalism relates to a series of issues dealing with the family. If there is a classic statement of a modern liberal view on this subject, it is those sections of *The Third Way* by Anthony Giddens which deal with these issues. One of the trends that he claims is very clear in our society is the decline of the traditional family, the rise in divorce and the growth of single-parent families. These, he believes in turn, are the result of the increasing equality between the sexes, the entry of women into the labour force in a major way, changes in sexual behaviour and expectations and the changing relationship between home and work. His conclusion is that because these are such profound processes of change the return to the traditional family or even the idealistic family of the 1950s is a non-starter.

The future for the family which he then proposes is 'the democratic family'. As public democracy has been extended, so the family has and certainly should become increasingly democratised. In the public sphere democracy involves formal equality, individual rights, public discussion of issues without resort to violence, and authority that is negotiated, not based on tradition. The ideal he proposes for the democratic family is emotional and sexual equality, the autonomy and mutual rights of each partner, decision making through communication, freedom from violence and life-long parental contracts. In the past he says that marriage and parenthood have always been thought of together, but in the de-traditionalised family, where having a child is a totally different kind of decision from in the past, the two are separate. 'Contractual commitment to a child should thus be separated from marriage and made by each parent as a binding matter of law.' The principles which underpin 'the democratic family' are not restricted to heterosexual relationships but apply just as strongly to homosexual ones as well.

From such examples, drawn from very different fields, it is not surprising that secular liberalism has been and continues to be the enemy of Conservatism. It has no respect for tradition, it has no objective standards of morality, and it has no anchor to give stability to the social order. It has an optimism about politics, economics and the social order based on reason and the autonomy and potential of the human person in which in the final analysis the individual is the supreme judge.

I would now like to consider one possible objection which may be made to the argument so far, namely that while the relationship between the Christian faith and a Conservative political philosophy is interesting as a matter of history, it is of limited relevance today. Britain is now a multi-religious society made up of Christians, Jews, Muslims, Sikhs and Hindus. Perhaps even more importantly, the process of secularisation has taken a heavy toll. The practice of the Christian religion, judged by the statistics on churchgoing, baptisms, confirmations, ordinations, religious marriages and funerals, is in unambiguous decline. Modern Britain therefore requires a modern Conservatism that is detached from its historic religious roots.

John Gray confidently declares that the great political fact of our age is the passing of Christianity, which he understands not as a variety of personal faith but as the unifying worldview of a culture. He pours scorn particularly on what he calls 'the fundamentalist project for the re-Christianisation of Western societies', which he says can be taken seriously by 'nobody with any sense of historical perspective'. He thunders on, confidently asserting that 'most of Britain is a post-religious, and in particular, a post-Christian society' and declaring that

> the current neo-fundamentalist clamour for a return to the traditional family [is] misconceived and frivolous in the highest degree. It expresses no serious concern for the needs of people in families, nor any understanding of the diverse forms in which the institution of the family is now to be found. Such vulgar clamour is symptomatic of contemporary conservative thought in the unreality of its perception of real people and their needs.

He raises issues that need to be addressed. Britain today is clearly a multi-religious society and it is important that there is freedom and space for people of all religious faiths. The irony, however, is that in terms of their approach to social questions people of different religious faiths have more in common with each other than they do with those who subscribe to secular liberalism. People of different religions value tradition, the family and religious schools. They are firmly opposed to the immoralism of Bloomsbury. They do not make a sharp distinction between private morality and public morality. The fact that Britain is a multi-religious society, far from undermining the need for a political philosophy to be grounded in religion, only strengthens it.

The claim, however, that Britain is a post-religious and post-Christian society needs to be challenged. The notion that we live in a post-religious society is simply not true. In the course of the twentieth century Max Weber's thesis regarding secularisation gained enormous ground. He had argued that with the advance of industrialisation, rationalisation, urbanisation and the spread of education and science, there would be no room left in our society for God and the supernatural. The consequence of these trends would be the decline of religion and the emergence of a secular society which would be pluralist, tolerant, uncommitted to any particular worldview and in which there would be a sharp distinction between private and public morality. It is a thesis that is no longer accepted by sociologists, and the reason is that it flies in the face of evidence documenting the continued strength of traditional religions, the growth of new-age religions and astrology, and the continuing importance of traditional religious belief in political debate. In the country in which secularisation might have been expected to have advanced furthest, namely America, a new book by Professor Robert Fogel, a Nobel laureate at the University of Chicago, describes the past forty to fifty years as the 'Fourth Great Awakening', namely a religious revival, comparable in its significance to the three other great religious awakenings in America, in the late eighteenth century, the mid-nineteenth century and the late nineteenth century. Professor Rodney Stark, a sociologist at Washington University, sums up the views of many of his colleagues when he says that the evidence 'leads to the conclusion that secularisation will not usher in a post-religious era. Instead it will lead repeatedly to a resupply of vigorous other worldly religious organisations by promoting revival.'

The case for Britain having become a post-Christian society is stronger but again the issue is far from simple. Statistics of official religious practices certainly suggest a major decline, as does the change in the law relating to abortion, divorce, homosexuality, Sunday trading, the lottery and so on. But against this there is the numerical strength of informal Christian practices such as prayer groups, the remarkable success of the Alpha course (which is an introductory course to the Christian faith), of the Spring Harvest Christian conferences, the continuing strength and significance of religion in Parliament (as part of which I would include the work of the CCF), the continued popularity of church schools, the fact that the language we are driven to use to explain the horrors of phenomena such as Dunblane, the murder of James Bulger and the Holocaust cannot avoid the category of evil, and the fact that a high percentage of the population when asked 'Do you believe in God?' answer 'Yes'.

When we move away from simple statistics the issue of assessing the vitality and vigour of a Christian society is more difficult. In attempting to do so T. S. Eliot made three distinctions which I find helpful. First he describes the Christian State, which is the emphasis given to the Christian religion in legislation, public administration and legal tradition. The Christian Community is that part of the population in which there exists a unified religious social code, which is ingrained even though it may consist of largely unconscious behaviour. This would be supported by the structure of a national church, religiously based education, and the organisation of society on a Christian basis, though he declines to develop this theme. Finally there is the Community of Christians, which might be conceived of as the Church within the Church, and which would consist of consciously and thoughtfully practising Christians – especially, Eliot remarked, those of intellectual and spiritual superiority. Such a community would not be an organisation, but something today we might loosely describe as a network, made up of both clergy (though not all clergy) and laity, having an identity of belief and aspiration, in all probability a common educational background, a common culture and who collectively would make up the 'conscious mind and the conscience of the nation'.

In coming to a conclusion about whether Britain is a post-Christian society it is necessary to make a judgement on all of these. One can only hazard a guess: the Christian Community judged in terms of official statistics has certainly been in decline, as has to a lesser extent the Christian State. The irony is, however, that the Community of Christians remains strong, active and vigorous. Over recent decades the practice of the Christian religion has declined, but the debate over religion, especially in matters of public morality, remains strong and is one reason therefore why I would not come to a hasty conclusion in assessing the state of religion in British society. It is also because of this that I believe that groups such as the CCF have an important part to play in the life of this country.

Let me now turn to my final section. I believe that a Conservatism which is based on a religious worldview is as relevant to Britain today as it has been at any time since Burke wrote his *Reflections*. Let me give some examples.

Education is a subject that is difficult to separate from religion. Whether it is the teaching of religious instruction itself, the framework within which various intellectual disciplines are taught, or the values embodied in the culture of a school, it is impossible for a Christian to separate education from religion. This was why in 1811, the Church of England took a major step in the provision of education in England and Wales by setting up the National Society for Promoting the Education of the Poor in the Principles of the Established Church throughout England and Wales, at a time when there was no state provision. It was followed in the nineteenth century by the establishment of various Anglican teacher-training colleges to supply trained teachers. Today there are about 4,500 Church of England primary schools, roughly one fifth of the total number of primary schools in England, and 202 secondary schools, which account for only 4 per cent of this sector. There are nearly 2,100 Roman Catholic schools and a small number of Jewish and Muslim schools. In addition there are a considerable number of independent schools, probably less than 1,000 of which have a Christian foundation. Other than the independent schools, these are financed largely but not exclusively by taxpayers' money.

In addition to this, successive Education Acts have laid down specific religious duties for all schools: namely that the curriculum of a school should promote the spiritual, moral, cultural, mental and physical development of the pupils, that there should be arrangements for an act of collective worship on a daily basis, wholly, or mainly, of a broadly Christian character, and that the religious education of the school should reflect the religious tradition of Britain, which is in the main Christian, while taking into account the teaching and practices of the other principal religions in this country as well.

Church schools serve a much wider community than the children of church members, and include children of parents of no faith and of parents who belong to other churches and other religions. Judged by the demand for places, church schools must be considered successful. The reason for their success is that, apart from what might be expected from any good school, they teach moral principles and values based on the Christian religion, governors and staff are committed to creating an ethos in the school in which Christian character is held up as virtue, and by respecting the Christian calendar they help children understand the traditions and public festivals of our country which have extended over centuries. The ethos of a church school was put successfully recently by one head teacher: 'We don't admit children, we admit families.'

It is because of the demand for such schools that the Archbishop of Canterbury established the Church Schools Review Group under the chairmanship of Lord Dearing to look into the future of church schools in early 1999. In its interim report, published in July 1999, it noted that there are major cities and towns such as Bournemouth, Brighton, Gloucester, Newcastle upon Tyne, Plymouth and Sheffield without a maintained C of E secondary school and other areas without primary church schools, and recommended that 100 additional Church of England secondary schools should be established. Their view was that these schools should have a substantial core of Christian teachers and pupils from Christian families so that they could be living Christian communities. This is a very significant initiative and in my judgement deserves the support of all Christian people as an attempt to restore the importance of faith, morality and the sacred in our society. One example of a recently created Christian school is the Emmanuel City Technology College in Gateshead, which was the only city technology college established on a religious basis. It has achieved remarkable academic success, coming second in the GCSE league tables, quite apart from the emphasis placed on developing the whole person. It is convinced that its success is due to its emphasis on Christian values and standards being integral to the life of the school.

A second area in which a religiously based Conservatism is relevant has to do with the family. From a theological point of view one could argue that the institution of the family is part of the created order, that marriage not cohabitation should be the norm for society, and that gay marriage is an oxymoron. From a political point of view, however, the case will need to be argued primarily on the basis of research evidence. It has been becoming increasingly clear for some time now that the body of research in this area supports a number of important conclusions:

First, studies show that a stable marriage, with two parents of different sexes, is the best environment in which to raise children. It results in superior educational attainment, less probability of being involved in crime or being the victim of domestic violence, less likelihood of teenage pregnancy, less likelihood of divorce should children marry in later life and a greater probability of getting higher paid work. Research also confirms that the effects on children of divorce and separation are much greater than has previously been appreciated, resulting especially in low self-esteem for the children themselves. Added to this, young children have been shown to suffer from spending long periods in day care, while surveys of working mothers suggest that many would prefer the greater choice that a more even-handed tax and benefit system might provide.

William Hague's commitment to reform the tax and benefit system to support the institution of marriage is an important step in the right direction and will ease the present burden imposed on parents in bringing up children. It should be welcomed not just by Conservatives but by anyone who has an interest in strengthening the family. This is not an attack on single parents, who have one of the most difficult and emotionally draining jobs to do, but it is simply a recognition that ideally children are better off with two parents and that families committed to marriage are the most stable. Such a policy would also, as Jill Kirby has so convincingly argued, ensure that mothers are not under financial pressure to return to work before their children are ready and would therefore be a boost to valuing motherhood. In this connection I believe that the establishment of the Renewing One Nation team to develop an inclusive Conservatism is important.

My final example is the part that religiously based charities could play in the strengthening of civil society. Nobody doubts the needs that exist today. Again William Hague said recently, reminiscent of Wilberforce's concern,

> no decent society can be at peace with itself when so many children are excluded from prosperity and opportunity. No decent society can just sit back and watch as drug abuse spreads to the school playground. No decent society can be indifferent as more children grow up in homes where no father has ever been present. And no decent society can allow the same communities to suffer long term unemployment, generation after generation.

Some of these problems can only be tackled by governments. Even when there is a private option, the public sector may have a role to play. I have known at first hand over recent years social service staff of a local authority who have provided an excellent personal, caring service. We have to be careful in denouncing the role of government as a service provider carte blanche. Nevertheless, there is within the world of religious charities a potential to be tapped that could be extremely helpful. It may not be as great as some imagine but it is certainly an option that needs to be explored. We should not expect it to be a panacea, and in any event some organisation will have to accept overall responsibility for identifying those needing help and not receiving it. But the innumerable examples from the history of this country over the past 200 years suggests that instead of simply paying taxes and assuming the state will do the rest, we ourselves will have to accept greater personal responsibility for the needs of our neighbours.

Let me now sum up and draw some conclusions. The case I have sought to argue is that since the Conservative Party was founded, nearly 200 years ago, the case for Conservatism has been presented as inextricably bound up with a religious perspective. I have tried to show how Christianity underpins a reforming Conservatism, which values tradition, believes in an objective basis for morality, wishes to strengthen civil society, is sceptical of any attempt to realise through politics heaven on earth, but is strongly committed to addressing the needs of the poor and remedying injustice.

The danger we face today is to be seduced in the name of tolerance by a libertarian social philosophy, which contains no objective standards of morality and which will lead, through the abuse of freedom and neglect of responsibility, to a multiplicity of social problems. Ultimately, and this is the real irony, this would require a more authoritarian framework for society to redress the chaos which such a society will inevitably produce. Conservatism has always stood against libertarianism, as the negation of everything it stands for. If the Conservative Party were to become libertarian it would in my judgement be the end of the Conservative Party as we have known it.

Let me be very clear in what I am saying. No individual can play God. We have no right to judge another person's private lifestyle. But in terms of public morality and the preservation of those institutions on which the future of our society depends we are entitled to argue for what is in the best interests of society itself. As Christians we will have a religious basis for our views, though increasingly the currency of political debate will mean that it will only be accepted on the basis of what works.

This is a lecture in honour of William Wilberforce and, in reading about him and what he wrote, I have been particularly struck by his humility and piety. We will continue to debate the pros and cons of his policies, but his abiding legacy is that above everything else, each one of us should show something personally of the love of God to those around us and, as we are reminded in the picture of the final judgment in St Matthew, especially to those in need, the hungry, the thirsty, the sick, the naked, those in prison. Let us remember, finally, the words of the Shepherd: 'In as much as you did it unto one of the least of these my brethren you did it unto me.'

2002

Iain Duncan Smith

William Wilberforce was driven by the idea that every man and woman on earth possesses infinite dignity. Made in the image of God, every person matters; every person who ever lived bore the imprint of eternity. This idea burned within Wilberforce and inspired his whole life, but it was the evil trade in slaves that most offended his belief in humanity. In parliamentary debates he described the terrible waste of life caused by thousands of slaves being transported across oceans in cramped and disease-ridden ships.

Wilberforce believed that all human life was cheapened by the treatment of slaves, and saw a close connection between the slave trade and the inhuman treatment of many children in Britain's major cities. He stood up for his beliefs despite the hatred and ridicule that were poured upon him. For more than forty years he faced powerful vested interests, but never wavered in his fight against the obscenity of slavery.

I want to dedicate this fifth William Wilberforce Address to the same idea that inspired Wilberforce two centuries ago. My politics are drawn from the eternal Christian principle that every individual person is infinitely valuable – but this is not the whole story. Christianity is a religion of community, with love of God and neighbour at its heart; without community, individuals are fractions of themselves. We cannot fulfil our humanity without the help of others, or without helping others.

Solidarity with others comes from, and creates, community. By community I do not mean the state, I mean each of us and all of us. We are commanded to love our neighbour, and that responsibility cannot be surrendered to the state. Each of us has responsibilities as parents and neighbours that only we can fulfil. People cannot fulfil their humanity when their responsibilities are taken from them.

Some people believe that a bigger role for government is the only way to compensate for the weakness of society's free institutions, but this belief risks feeding a vicious cycle of family and community breakdown. Because the increased power of the state is not just the wrong solution – it is at the very heart of the problem.

The bigger the state becomes, the more it crowds out people and undermines the natural institutions that generate our society's wealth and values. This doesn't mean government has no part to play, but we must be clear that government's role is to serve, not to control. Conservatives believe in strengthening the relationships within society rather than increasing the power of the state, and I believe in trusting people, not politicians. Tonight, I want to share these beliefs and talk about how they relate to three fundamental policy objectives: the strengthening of the family, the renewal of society and international poverty relief.

The most fundamental institution of any free and sustainable society is the family. Within the family, children learn about friendship, sharing and forgiveness. Children's other-regarding instincts are strengthened so that they inform and condition their instinctive self-regarding instincts. Through the memories of parents and grandparents, children gain a unique sense of identity and so wisdom and wealth flow down the generations.

Much of the joy of being a parent or grandparent is knowing

that our life's experiences have been given to our children. At a material level, parents work and save not only for themselves but for their children's futures. The overwhelming benefit of being in a family, however, is the stability it brings, a fact that was powerfully documented by Jill Kirby in her paper 'Broken Hearts'. Jill's work makes it clear that a whole range of social challenges will defeat us if we do not strengthen the family.

If vulnerable young people are ever to escape from the conveyor belt to crime they need better parenting. If we are to maintain an educated workforce, children need to be raised in homes where learning is encouraged. If we are to renew community life, families must become strong enough to look beyond their own needs.

As a society we must help families to flourish, but our society is not helping families; the tax and benefits system is actually weighted against the family. Such discrimination needs to be addressed by politicians, but some politicians are frightened of even talking about the family. They think that marriage is less valuable to children and society because people often struggle to live up to the ideals of marriage.

Politicians' relationships fail in the same way that relationships sadly fail in the rest of society, and so some politicians avoid using the 'M' word, as if it is some kind of social expletive, and speak as though they give extra help to single-parent families simply by failing to give any support to married couples.

However, the statistics speak for themselves: 80 per cent of young people still aspire to marriage but find that aspiration difficult to realise. Most families in Britain do still succeed and stay together, and Conservatives cannot truly claim to be the party of aspiration if we do not support the popular aspiration to form lasting relationships. Governments already support a range of aspirations that are good for individuals and wider society. Starting a business, saving for the future or studying for a career are all incentivised in various ways.

Why, then, is support for the aspiration to raise the next generation so inadequate?

Couples who seek support for their relationship, or parental education, should have access to it. Of course, government cannot provide such help itself, but it can resource those who do. I am also determined that we should learn from European countries that do not take hard-working families for granted. They have created tax and benefit systems that recognise the social benefits of marriage.

It is, of course, true that many people do not make a success of the relationships in which they once invested so much hope. Often these relationships fail for reasons beyond people's control, but being the party of aspiration does not mean that we should not help these people and their children. They need all of our help.

The family is society's most basic unit, but society also includes faith communities, voluntary organisations, local schools and public service professionals. Society is defined by the civilities, traditions and institutions that bind people together and prepare them for the future. Faith-inspired charities have a remarkable record of tackling social challenges, and Conservatives want to help them and other voluntary organisations.

Schools are at the heart of local neighbourhoods, and they succeed when their head teachers have the power and flexibility to lead. Conservatives will give head teachers more freedom – particularly over vital disciplinary matters – and we will give parents the opportunity to establish new schools at the taxpayers' expense if they are not satisfied with existing provision. This will give voluntary groups and faith communities unprecedented opportunities to establish schools that reinforce the values of a child's home.

Morale among society's public service professionals has never been lower. Their enthusiasm and dedication is being drained by a system that attempts to micro-manage their work and prevents them from actively serving local people. Conservative reforms will be focused on ensuring that healthcare, education and policing are delivered on a human scale.

Conservatives will champion localism. When we talk about decentralisation it will not be to a new tier of politicians and bureaucrats. Instead, we will set free professionals and local communities. But it's not enough to focus all our efforts on problems at home when the challenges of the world's poorest countries are so great. The parable of the Good Samaritan reminds us that people outside of our borders are still our neighbours. Our neighbour is not just the person who lives in the next house or the next street – although we do have a special duty to them. Civilisation as a whole is diminished when a child dies from malnutrition or from a curable disease. The old ways of fighting poverty in the developing world may have failed, but this is no excuse for walking away from our responsibilities to our neighbours.

Conservative international development policy must be informed by a rediscovery of the same principles that are reshaping the Conservative Party's domestic agenda, and we must invest in those institutions that build people up. In the past, much aid expenditure has been wasted on grand projects when basic needs such as women's health and education were being neglected. Massive construction projects have at times damaged the natural environment because of insensitive applications of technology.

Many development charities have pioneered new approaches to sustainable development and poverty-fighting. These approaches are at their most successful when they work on a human scale with local charitable and community groups in the countries concerned. Again, success is rooted in trusting people, and small loans entrusted to women and families often produce spectacular results. More of the UK's development budget should be spent through non-governmental organisations.

Through our commitment to help the world's poorest we strengthen our humanity in practical and profound ways; our moral character and national self-interest come together. Extremes of poverty breed the failed states of tomorrow and these states, in turn, breed terrorism, drug-trafficking and hazardous patterns of migration. Effective international development policy will tackle poverty, hunger and disease in the developing world and at the same time it will protect the global environment and enhance our security.

Many of you here have contributed to the CCF's Listening to Britain's Churches consultations and, I hope, have witnessed how the fellowship has already represented your views to the Conservative Party. The days when politicians could simply announce policies to a waiting world and then impose them upon people are over.

I have recently visited a number of schools and community projects, among them two inspirational Christian initiatives. In Manchester, last Monday, I visited the Message Trust; a few days later, in Cardiff, I spent time with Care for the Family. Both prove that people of spirit can overcome the deepest and most intractable social challenges, and fundamental to their work is the same high view of the human person held by Wilberforce.

For at least two decades political discussion has been distorted by a false analysis of the way we live. A zealous individualism was frequently seen as the opposite of the state when, in reality, both tend to feed each other. A lonely individualism cuts people off from the people-sized and values-generating institutions that build a compassionate society; it paves the way for a bigger state to pick up the pieces of neglected children and broken communities.

Conservatives have embarked upon a journey of rediscovering our deepest beliefs, because the values and institutions of society have been neglected by politicians. My mission is to renew their strength and vitality, to ensure that politics serves the British people and their way of life. Cardinal Cormac Murphy-O'Connor recently said of the democratic political system: 'It needs people of the highest integrity and ideals to bring to fruition the principles upon which it is based – principles of fairness, freedom, mutual respect and democratic accountability.'

Wilberforce was a member of Parliament before he became a Christian. When he found his faith he almost gave up his seat and like many enthusiastic believers he considered becoming ordained, but he was persuaded to stay in politics by John Newton, the writer of 'Amazing Grace'. Before becoming a Christian, Newton had been the cruellest of slave owners, and he persuaded Wilberforce to stay in politics and champion his Christian views in Parliament. That is my invitation to you today.

There has never been a better time to be politically involved. The democratic opportunities within each of the mainstream political parties are enormous. Political service is a noble expression of an individual's commitment to his or her neighbour and to the common good. William Wilberforce changed history with his parliamentary battle against the evil slave trade and there are still great battles to be fought today: the battle to give every child a home where they are loved and feel secure; the battle to free our streets of crime and drugs; the battle to create a society where people of every faith, background and colour are welcomed.

These timeless ideals have been ill served by failed ideologies, but there is no room in the Christian worldview for despondency. People can make a difference in politics just as they can in their families and communities. Perhaps a 21st-century Wilberforce is sitting in this room tonight. Following in that great man's footsteps is a worthy calling for any Christian. I leave you with that challenge.

2004

David Lidington

In 1833, both Houses of Parliament suspended business in order to attend the funeral of William Wilberforce. His pallbearers numbered two royal dukes, the Lord Chancellor, the Speaker of the House of Commons and four peers.

Wilberforce had served in Parliament for nearly fifty years. During that time he held no official position in government or the country, yet he achieved more than most members of Parliament dare dream of. His monument, in the north aisle of Westminster Abbey, bears an epitaph probably written by Macaulay: 'In an age and country fertile in great and good men, he was among the foremost of those who fixed the character of their times because to high and various talents, to warm benevolence, and to universal candour, he added the abiding eloquence of a Christian life.'

The late Enoch Powell wrote, in his biography of Joseph Chamberlain, that 'all political lives, unless they are cut off in midstream at a happy juncture, end in failure, because that is the nature of politics and of human affairs'. The life of William Wilberforce was a triumphant and glorious exception to that rule. William Wilberforce is remembered and celebrated above all for his campaign to abolish slavery and the slave trade, a victory described by G. M. Trevelyan as 'one of the turning events in the history of the world'. But his philanthropic impulse led him also to take up causes such as prison reform and improving hospitals. He was a founder member of the RSPCA, and his example inspired succeeding generations of his compatriots to devote their energies to humanitarian causes and to social reform.

Wilberforce lived in the days before parliamentary debates were accurately reported and published, so we can only glimpse the impact that his oratory had on an audience. Pitt declared that: 'Of all men I ever knew, Wilberforce has the greatest natural eloquence'. Like all the best speakers, Wilberforce knew how to select the word or phrase that was best suited to those whom he was seeking to persuade, and he knew how to command the attention of the House of Commons. George Canning commented that Wilberforce 'understands thoroughly the tactics of debates and . . . knows what will carry the House along with him'.

Both his contemporaries and his biographers agree that Wilberforce was the most lovable and loving of men. He had no airs or graces and seems to have been blessed with an ability to find joy or serenity even at times of political or personal crisis. My favourite anecdote of Wilberforce is one recounted by Marianne Thornton, whose father Henry was Wilberforce's friend. She recalled how, as a young child, she met the great man.

> He was as restless and volatile as a child himself, and during the grave discussions that went on between him and my father and others, he was most thankful to refresh himself by throwing a ball or a bunch of flowers at me, or opening the glass door and going off with me for a race on the lawn 'to warm his feet'.

Wilberforce was no dour puritan. In seeking to improve the lot of humanity, he never forgot that loving one's neighbour begins with loving individual men, women and children – not a bad lesson for any of us, but perhaps especially for those of us who work in government or Parliament, to hold in our hearts. No modern political party has the right to claim a patent on Wilberforce's name or his political legacy, but Conservatives have for two centuries looked to his memory for inspiration. Wilberforce is a pre-eminent example of the truth that nations and communities are not helpless in the face of impersonal economic or social forces, that individual witness and effort can make a difference to the sum of human happiness. His emphasis on the importance of personal responsibility, conscience and action find an echo in much contemporary Conservative thinking about social policy.

My intention this evening is to ask whether it would be possible for a Christian politician today to achieve what Wilberforce did. How have the far-reaching intellectual and social changes that have taken place during the past 200 years affected the place of faith in political discourse? How can we draw on the Conservative tradition in British politics to respond to this challenge?

Wilberforce saw his campaigns to abolish slavery and to reform manners as a form of Christian ministry. He had, as a young man, wrestled in his mind over whether political ambition was actually compatible with his deepening commitment to the Christian faith. In his diary, he wrote: 'As soon as I reflected seriously upon these subjects, the deep guilt and ingratitude of my past life forced itself upon me in the strongest colours and I condemned myself for having wasted my precious time and opportunities and talents.' He contemplated withdrawing altogether from public life.

It was William Pitt who helped persuade him otherwise. In 1785, he wrote to his friend from Downing Street. After assuring Wilberforce he would never think lightly of his moral or religious motives, he added that he feared Wilberforce was deluding himself 'into principles which have but too much tendency to counteract your own object, and to render your virtues and your talents useless both to yourself and mankind'. He continued: 'If a Christian may act in the several relations of life, must he seclude himself from all to become so? Surely the principles as well as the practice of Christianity are simple, and lead not to meditation only, but to action.' Could such an exchange take place today?

In one sense, yes; there are MPs of all political parties who see their parliamentary and political work as ministry to which they have been called. What is profoundly different today is the intellectual and moral climate within which Christians and politicians live. An eighteenth- or early nineteenth-century parliamentarian formed his opinions and decided on his actions within a spiritual and ethical frame of reference that, for all but a handful, was exclusively Christian. Richard Hooker's maxim that, in England, 'one society is both Church and Commonwealth' would still have been considered true by most parliamentarians, as well as by most clergy.

Our age is predominantly secular. Arguments nowadays will not succeed simply because they rest on Christian doctrine or are inspired by a sense of Christian mission. Indeed, Christianity sometimes finds it hard to get a hearing at all. This is the culmination of a trend that has been established for about a century and a half. Within just a few years of Wilberforce's death, the teaching and the constitutional position of the Church of England and of the Christian faith generally was being challenged by nothing short of an intellectual revolution. Matthew Arnold, in his poem *Dover Beach*, marked the change in elegiac tones.

The Sea of Faith
Was once, too, at the full, and round earth's shore
Lay like the folds of a bright girdle furled.
But now I only hear
Its melancholy, long, withdrawing roar,

Retreating, to the breath
Of the night-wind, down the vast edges drear
And naked shingles of the world.

Most obviously, the challenge to religion came from science, not only from Darwin but also from the insights of geologists and palaeontologists. But every bit as radical were the implications for the Church of political reform. Representative government rested on the principle that all were entitled to equal treatment under the law. If there were political equality, how could religious inequality be justified? If all people, whatever their faith, were entitled to schooling, to have their marriage recognised by the law and to be buried decently after death, then surely a non-denominational or secular state should intervene to ensure that these civil rights were indeed available.

When you look back at the parliamentary history of the nineteenth century, it is striking how many important political controversies touched on matters of religion. Education, civil marriage and burial are just three examples. The Test and Corporation Acts, which excluded Protestant dissenters from municipal office, were repealed in 1828. Catholic emancipation took place only after years of political battles. Rothschild was first elected to the Commons in 1847, but had to wait eleven years until the law was changed to allow him to take his seat without swearing an explicitly Christian oath. Tithes, eligibility to become a fellow of Oxford or Cambridge and the status of the Anglican Church in Wales and Ireland should be added to the list. These were not scholastic disputations, but hard-fought political battles. The young Gladstone actually resigned office over Peel's decision to give a grant to the Roman Catholic college at Maynooth.

The most striking contrast between Wilberforce's age and our own is the way in which Christianity, and indeed religious faith more generally, has now been pushed to the margins of public debate. Of course there are some good reasons why the language of political discourse has changed. Politicians (and, for that matter, bishops and other church leaders) ought to be very cautious before claiming divine approval for a particular policy. As the late Lord Hailsham once put it: 'Most political judgements are matters of degree, fact and opinion and have no bearing at all on the salvation of individual souls or the verities enshrined in the Nicene Creed.' I would be hard pressed to search out some Biblical or doctrinal premise which would lead ineluctably to a particular policy position on electronic voting or the location of speed cameras, to take two subjects on which I have voted in Parliament during the past week.

But I believe that we are now in danger of getting into the position where it is regarded as almost unseemly to bring religious commitments and religious criteria into political debate at all. Lord Melbourne, after listening to an evangelical sermon, exclaimed: 'Things are coming to a pretty pass when religion is allowed to invade private life.' In our time, the reverse is the case. Our society is now getting into a situation in which the introduction of religion into public life and public debate is regarded as impertinent, embarrassing or just plain irrelevant.

Every cloud has its silver lining, and the 2001 Census reported that just over three-quarters of the population identified themselves as having a religion. A total of 72 per cent, more than 42 million people, described themselves (or were described by their parents) as Christian. Muslims, the second largest faith community, account for 2.7 per cent of the population, or nearly 1.6 million people. About 16 per cent of people stated that they had no religion. This category included all those who described themselves as atheists, agnostics, heathens and Jedi knights.

But it is difficult to draw too much comfort from those figures when you set them alongside what we see in daily life. There are some striking exceptions, but overall attendance at church continues to fall. People are choosing to spend time on Sunday playing or watching sport or shopping, rather than going to worship. What was once a common Christian literary heritage has also been eroded. Bible stories, and the language and phrases of the King James Bible, the Book of Common Prayer and popular hymns are becoming accessible to fewer and fewer people. A decline in religious observance has reduced the stock of cultural references that are shared by all.

Conservatives have found these changes in our society particularly troubling. Partly, this is simply because a conservative disposition leads one to be sceptical of change, but it is also, at least in part, due to the historic identification of the Conservative Party with established Christianity.

It is simply not the case that the Conservative Party, unlike our sister parties in the European Christian Democrat tradition, has always been secular in outlook. Until very recently in our party's history, defence of and support for the Christian faith was integral to what it meant to be a Conservative.

Let me give a few examples. Edmund Burke, in *Reflections on the Revolution in France*, wrote:

> We know and feel inwardly that religion is the basis of civil society, and the source of all good and comfort . . . All persons possessing any portion of power ought to be strongly and awefully impressed with an idea that they act in trust; and that they are to account for that conduct in that trust to the one great master, author and founder of society.

Disraeli, speaking in Aylesbury in 1861, declared: 'The most powerful principle which governs man is the religious principle . . . A wise government, allying itself with religion, would as it were consecrate society, and sanctify the state.' Three years later, in

Oxford, he reiterated the point. 'Upon our acceptance of that divine interpretation for which we are indebted to the Church, and of which the Church is the guardian, all sound and salutary legislation depends. That truth is the only security for salvation, and the only guarantee of real progress.'

These were not sentiments that died with Queen Victoria. They were repeated in two classic twentieth-century expositions of Conservative philosophy. Lord Hugh Cecil, in his study *Conservatism*, published in 1912, asserted that

> defence of the Church against attack, either on its established position or on its endowments, is an essential part of the work of Conservatism. Heir of Toryism as it is, it stands for the Church and for the formal recognition of religion by the state . . . Conservatism insists on the national acceptance of Christianity, and desires to reconcile that acceptance with complete toleration of all sorts of opinions on religious matters . . . The championship of religion . . . is the most important of the functions of Conservatism. It is the keystone of the arch upon which the whole fabric rests.

As late as 1950, the Conservative Party's general election manifesto listed 'reverence for Christian ethics' as the first of five principles which were described as 'pillars on which we base our faith'. These were not just statements of personal witness, they were expressions of how the Conservative Party saw the relationship of faith and politics as integral to its view of the world. And they are not statements that one can imagine in a Conservative manifesto today.

Don't get me wrong, I am not here to recite some modern version of the Book of Lamentations, nor am I about to launch into a chorus of 'Fings ain't what they used to be'. The Christian Church for 2,000 years and the Conservative Party for a somewhat shorter period of time have proved remarkably adept at adjusting to social and political change. Christians in the West now have to operate in a world where the idea that political argument should have a Christian character and Christian motivation, far from being the norm, is considered a bit odd. At its most extreme, the tendency to shunt Christianity to the margins of public discourse springs from an aggressive secularism that derides religion as inimical to human liberty and progress. Some of the comments of Philip Pullman fall into this category, and only last week one columnist in *The Times* wrote that 'individual freedom depends on keeping religion firmly in its place'.

I have to admit that I can understand, to some extent, the grounds on which this line of argument is pursued. You don't even have to look outside our own country. Drive through north Belfast and you travel through residential estates that are in the same city but exist in different worlds. The most depressing sight that I have seen in Northern Ireland is the so-called peace line: 20-foot-high green metal fences to separate members of the two communities, and erected with the consent and support of local people. In places, the line literally divides one row of small back yards from another. On one side of the barrier, Irish tricolours are flown and murals on the gable ends of houses commemorate slain IRA 'volunteers'. A few yards away but on the other side of the fence, kerbstones are painted red, white and blue and the murals commemorate the Battle of the Boyne or show Oliver Cromwell crushing the Pope.

You don't even have to cross the Irish Sea. In cities such as Bradford and Oldham, Muslim and non-Muslim British citizens have chosen to live apart. Housing estates, shops and schools observe a kind of voluntary apartheid. No government has imposed segregation; people themselves have chosen to live their lives that way.

It is true, of course, that today the political battles in Northern Ireland are over national identity and the legitimacy of the state, rather than over ancient religious enmities. Three decades of vicious terrorism have left a legacy of grief, bitterness and resentment that will take at least a generation to overcome. It is also true that in Bradford, as in Belfast, poor housing, inadequate schools and drug-trafficking are fertile soil in which religious and ethnic tension and hostility can flourish. But we would be foolish to pretend that religion has had no part to play in creating the problems with which this country now has to grapple. And I believe that it is important that those of us who are committed Christians, and who believe that our faith is often traduced, understand the case made by those who see faith as the enemy of both freedom and peace.

However, much more widespread than hostility to religion is the belief that, while religion may not be harmful, faith and politics should be kept apart. Religion is something that is fine for consenting adults in private, but should not be part of public life. It is not only politicians on the left who are tempted in this direction. Look back at the celebrated Church of England report of the 1980s, *Faith in the City*. I thought at the time, and think now, that it was an unbalanced document, which placed quite unwarranted confidence in the capacity of government to cure deep-seated social problems. It deserved criticism, and more generally I believe that church leaders (lay or clerical) who make political statements should accept, perhaps even welcome, vigorous challenge and debate. What was wrong was the charge that in publishing that report, Christian leaders were intervening in a debate in which they had no right to participate.

Some of the reactions from our party were a bit reminiscent of the attitude of Queen Elizabeth I, who, when in the Chapel Royal and hearing the preacher starting to talk about the need of Her Majesty to think to the future of her realm by securing succession, rose from her pew, flung her prayer book at the offending clergyman and yelled at him: 'To your text, Sir Priest! To your text!'

When it comes to more recent statements by Christian leaders on political subjects, I support some, I disagree with others. My chief criticism would actually be that the bishops of the Church of England, who have the rare privilege of seats in our legislature, are too often absent from the Upper House, even when issues are debated on which a religious perspective would be of great value.

How then should a Christian engaged in politics and, more specifically, a Christian who is also a Conservative, respond to the example of William Wilberforce today? Let me suggest three themes.

First, we need to reassert that religious faith cannot be confined to private life, that a religious perspective has much to contribute to public discourse. All three Abrahamic faiths teach that obedience to God has profound implications for how we live our lives in the world. Christians know that our first loyalty should be to God, rather than to earthly institutions, but believe too that the Incarnation was the ultimate expression of God's unending and unconditional love for the world that he had created. Loving your neighbour is not an abstract idea but a commitment that has to be carried out in the place where we live and the time that we are born. Political activity is one way in which to show that love in action.

Last Thursday, I went back from Westminster to my Aylesbury constituency to attend a meeting in St Mary's parish church. It was a meeting organised by the local Friends of the Earth, supported by the National Farmers' Union, to discuss the implications of GM technology for food, farming and the environment. More than 100 people attended. Opposing speakers were listened to with attention and respect. Questions were serious. There was a refreshing absence of political point-scoring. Yet I picked up one or two grumbles that it was wrong for such an event to take place in a church. I disagree. What could possibly be a more appropriate venue for a debate that touched upon profound issues about human stewardship of nature and our responsibilities to future generations?

Perhaps inevitably, political debates today are dominated by what is immediate. What subject will capture the headlines tomorrow? What topic does the latest poll tell us that the electorate is worried about?

What can we achieve given the deadlines imposed by the parliamentary year, the budget cycle or the timetable for elections? None of this is improper. It is good that politicians have to be sensitive to the concerns of the people. The downside is that both historical perspective and thought for the long-term future are often absent. The Church and other faith groups can bring to political debate an understanding of human nature, of social relationships and of mankind's relations with the rest of creation that can help to restore the balance.

Often, Christians will find ready allies among members of other faiths. A few months ago, I became involved in the margins of the row about the ban on religious notices, including one for the parish carol service, being displayed at the public library in High Wycombe. It turned out that the restriction had been introduced about twenty years ago and had been intended to deal with genuine worries about extremists and I am glad to say that this over-rigid policy has now been amended to provide for librarians to exercise their common sense. What was remarkable about this particular political squall was that while some commentators argued that the ban should be upheld in order not to offend other faiths, the High Wycombe Mosque called publicly for the ban to be rescinded. Whether we are talking about library notices or about religious education in schools, members of all faiths have a common interest in making sure that the spiritual dimension of human experience is not written out of the script of public life in this country.

I hope that we will see more Christians willing to involve themselves in politics, and that a large number will take an extra step and become active members of a political party. It can sometimes be a bit depressing to go to a Christian meeting, hear from people who are fired up about poverty or international development or care of the dying, and find that nobody there is actually a member of any party or has any intention of joining one. If the Church is to have a real voice in public debate, then more committed Christians need to look beyond the 'holy huddle' and engage with the flawed world of councils and parliaments.

Second, we have to rebut the accusation that faith is intolerant. Yes, great evil has been done in the name of religion, but deeds of dreadful wickedness have also been done in the name of racial superiority, national interest or dynastic ambition. Genocidal tyrannies such as Soviet Russia, Maoist China and Pol Pot's Cambodia were avowedly and militantly atheist and persecuted viciously the practice of religion.

Conservatives can bring something else to this debate, something that is closely linked to Christian teaching. To be a Conservative is to be sceptical. Conservatives believe that all people and all human institutions are fallible. We are instinctively suspicious of political ideologies that claim to have the answer to mankind's troubles. We believe that government is necessary but that the powers and the scope of government should be limited. This is partly because the exercise of power is tempting and tends to corrupt, but also because governments, whatever their political colour and however well intentioned, are composed of imperfect human beings who inevitably make lots of mistakes.

Scepticism is the ally of tolerance and pluralism. It prompts humility because it accepts that human judgement is imperfect and so concedes the possibility that our own political convictions, no matter how deeply held, may in fact be wrong. Every man and woman involved in public life should from time to time examine his thinking and say, in the words of Oliver Cromwell, 'I beseech you, in the bowels of Christ, think it possible that ye may be mistaken'.

Scepticism and humility can help to overcome the mistrust that divides different religious communities. A Christian's awareness of his own sinfulness should make him hesitate before condemning others. In Northern Ireland, individual clergy, both Protestant and Catholic, have used the respect in which they are held within their respective traditions to reach out to political parties and even to paramilitary groups in efforts to bring about reconciliation. At some times of crisis, clergy have been the only intermediaries trusted by both sides.

Terrorism in Northern Ireland has left deep wounds. There must be a real danger now that atrocities carried out by terrorists claiming, wickedly, to act on behalf of Islam, will cause equal harm to community relations in cities throughout Britain. I believe that a grave responsibility falls on believers to take the lead in building mutual respect and understanding, even where there is profound disagreement. There are signs of hope. The Maimonides Foundation, a charity established to promote reconciliation between Jews and Muslims living in the United Kingdom, has initiated inter-faith meetings between religious leaders, dialogues between student groups on university campuses and a football coaching scheme (supported by Arsenal FC) for up to 100 Muslim and Jewish children.

In my own patch, local church leaders and the imam of the Aylesbury Mosque have met to discuss their faith and have attended each others' services. The imam has joined the chaplaincy team at the local young offenders' institution. He also came to the town mayor's civic carol service to speak a brief message of goodwill at Christmas from the Muslim community to their Christian neighbours; perhaps a small gesture, but one that was significant and moving. It also told me that neither Christians nor Muslims have to deny or dilute their faith for there to be trust and mutual respect between them.

Rather more challenging was the hour that I spent at the mosque to explain my reasons for supporting the war in Iraq and to answer questions. I can't pretend that the meeting finished in agreement but I hope that it concluded with a measure of greater understanding of each other's position. I certainly thought that it was my duty to accept the invitation. It is genuine, deep and principled disagreement that tests a relationship, whether between individuals or communities.

The world after 9/11 has left British Muslims feeling isolated and beleaguered. Yet it is vital, in the interests both of community relations in our own country and of overcoming the evil of international terrorism, that we are able to demonstrate that the real gulf is not between Christianity and Islam, but between honest believers of both faiths and a minority of ruthless and fanatical killers who are the foes of both. Al-Qaeda has already murdered thousands of Muslim men, women and children.

I would like to see Christian Conservatives take a lead reaching out to our Muslim fellow citizens. We understand that in a free and democratic society, people are quite entitled to oppose the war. Opposition to the war does not make someone a supporter of Saddam Hussein or al-Qaeda. Equally, supporting military action to remove Saddam Hussein or to strike at terrorist groups does not turn you into an enemy of Islam.

My third theme is that we need to show that faith is not something reserved for a small band gathered together on Sunday morning, but that it is a force for good in society as a whole. The Conservative tradition in Britain sees the collective life of human societies as something much richer and more subtle than the relationship between the individual and the state. Men and women can find their identity in numerous different collective organisations. It is quite possible to see yourself simultaneously as belonging to your family, your neighbourhood, a football club, the parent–teachers association, a reading group and a choral society, perhaps even a political party or a church.

These voluntary collective organisations, what Edmund Burke termed 'the little platoons', are a source of social strength. Because they are local and small scale, they can adapt much more nimbly to the particular and changing needs of individuals and neighbourhoods than can any agency of the state. They are free to go beyond the Whitehall rulebook that inevitably constrains the action of civil servants and local government officers.

The 'little platoons' also have a moral strength that derives from their voluntary nature. The activities of government are financed out of taxation. They depend, ultimately, upon the power of the state to coerce its citizens. One of the dangers in the growth of the state in modern societies is that as government intrudes more and more into different areas of life, it undermines citizenship. If it is always government that rushes in to solve problems (or at least says that it is doing so), people are more inclined to think that their civic duty has been completed with their tax return. A thriving voluntary sector is a sign that civic responsibility has not been quenched.

Many of the longest-established and some of the most innovative voluntary organisations in modern Britain are faith based. The majority are Christian, but there are Muslim, Jewish, Hindu and Sikh organisations as well.

Often they can provide not just help with money but the love and emotional support that so many people in our country desperately need. Think of the exhausted mother, living in a crime-ridden estate, desperate to keep her son off drugs and out of trouble; or an elderly widow, whose husband had always taken care of financial decisions, now trying to find her way through the bewildering maze of the social security system. They will both want practical help and advice, but also at times a cup of tea and a sympathetic arm around the shoulder, and those are things that even the most dedicated clerk in the Jobcentre or Inland Revenue office will not be able to give.

In my time as a member of Parliament, I have seen the work of the Shaftesbury Society, renewing homes and communities in east London, or Oasis, helping homeless people to find a fresh start in life. In my constituency, the churches in Princes Risborough took the lead in setting up Risborough Cares to keep the town's day centre going. Throughout the country, the quiet but utterly dedicated work of country clergy gave support to farmers and their families during the ordeal of the foot and mouth epidemic.

I want to see the entire voluntary sector grow and flourish. Yet so often government seems to raise up new obstacles. There are too many forms, too many government bidding schemes, each with its own rules. We need reforms that will make it easier for voluntary organisations, including some very little platoons, which cannot afford to hire accountants and consultants, to develop their good work.

It is dispiriting that a number of funding and grant-giving bodies still discriminate against faith-based organisations. I would agree that public money should not, as a rule, be used to support proselytising by any faith or denomination. Nor would I want a faith-based group to enjoy an unfair advantage in applying for money. Its proposal should be judged on its merits. But it is iniquitous to tell a church (or a synagogue, mosque, temple or gurdwara) that the only way to win official support, for even a superlative project, is to suppress all mention of the faith that inspires and sustains its works.

All of us hope to live lives that truly make a difference. We can never make the world perfect through politics, but politics gives us the opportunity that Wilberforce seized to make the world a better place, for at least some people at a particular time in human history.

The predominantly secular culture of our country makes it harder now than in the past for Christian argument and example to win an audience. But that challenge ought to spur us on to renewed effort, not a retreat into the holy huddle. The Conservative political tradition, with its humane scepticism, its confidence in local initiative and its belief in the capacity of free men and women to make a difference, has much to offer in that endeavour.

Few people have the gifts that were granted to William Wilberforce, but all can aspire to demonstrate, in some way, that 'abiding eloquence of a Christian life' for which we celebrate his memory this evening.

2005

Canon Andrew White

Like, I am sure, many here, I have lived in awe of William Wilberforce since childhood, and some of my earliest childhood memories are of drawing him and making clay models of him. Yes, I was a strange child. Having been a curate in Battersea Rise, and a vicar in Clapham South, I lived with the stories of the Clapham Sect. Indeed, when I was a Wandsworth Tory councillor, I had in my ward the precise patch where Wilberforce once lived. He was a man of great faith who had an immense interest not just in his own land but in the international community. Thus his lifelong campaign against the slave trade.

It is commonly said that the complexities and threats of the Middle East involve the three 'I's: Israel/Palestine, Iraq and Iran. It will be the first two that I want to concentrate on this evening, though my conclusions apply as much to the situation in Iran as in the other two 'I's.

The whole Middle East is a profoundly religious place. It is the supposed birthplace of creation and the very heart of the beginning of civilisation. It is the area that salvation history begins in and it is here that the three great monotheistic faiths have their birth. It is also here that we see the beginnings of some of the religious violence that afflicts us to this day, from the time of the Hellenistic Empire, in the assaults against the Holy Temple in Jerusalem, through the Christian Crusades, to the role of Hamas and Islamic Jihad and the attacks against Shia mosques and churches in Iraq today.

Whether we like it or not these are profoundly religious acts of destruction, carried out by religious people often against religious people. If we, as religious people, continue to deny the role of religion in conflict this will prevent us from dealing with the root cause of such violence. Oliver McTernan's influential book *Violence in God's Name* sums up the issue in its very title. If we are to make progress in peace-making we must take seriously the religious issue at a political, diplomatic, academic and religious level. If religion is in part responsible for the instigation of violence, it has to be part of the cure.

So let's begin by looking at the Israeli–Palestinian conflict. Searching for peace in the Middle East is a well-worn occupation. For years diplomats and politicians have sought to find new ways of ending this long conflict between the children of Ishmael and Isaac. It has been a conflict of people and land mirroring, in a way, the very covenant first revealed to the patriarch Abraham. Despite this endless conflict and the various peace processes taking on names of places around the world – Oslo, Taba, Wye River and Camp David, to mention but a few – none of them took seriously the religious dimensions of the land that is called Holy.

The Middle East is one of the most religious regions of the world. Religious involvement in conflict is usually not positive and something we must try to avoid, yet pretending that it does not exist is almost as dangerous as religious bigotry itself. When it comes to the Israeli–Palestinian conflict there has been a growing religious dimension to the conflict.

The most recent intifada even carries the name of one of the most holy places in Islam, al-Aqsa. And as you look at the Israeli–

Palestinian conflict you immediately see how many of the pivotal issues have strong religious connections – land, Jerusalem and the holy places. The major concerns are as relevant to religious leaders as politicians.

As Ariel Sharon has said: 'To you as Christians this is the Holy Land, but to us as Jews this is the Promised Land,' quoting the Pope. To Muslims, it can be added, this is *waf* (Islamic territory), so that to the three main religious traditions in the land this is no ordinary place. Even for those outside of the Middle East, Israel arouses strong feelings. There are millions of Christians around the world, not least in America, who believe fervently that the state of Israel is the fulfilment of Biblical prophecy, and to mess with it is to challenge the very work of the Almighty. We know that this position influences the only superpower left in the world today to a considerable extent.

Rabbi Michael Melchior, a member of the Knesset and an Orthodox rabbi, has said that the big question that must be asked is 'What went wrong with all the other peace plans?' and one of the answers must surely be that they did not gain religious legitimisation. It was partly for this reason that, after the beginning of the second intifada, plans were made to bring together the key religious leaders of Israel and Palestine. The basis of the meeting was a document written secretly in Jerusalem. Jewish, Christian and Muslim leaders were to come together to agree a joint commitment to work towards peace and against violence and terror. The meeting was to take place in Alexandria, Egypt, and the chairmen were to be the then Archbishop of Canterbury and the Grand Imam of al-Azhar, Sheikh Mohamed Sayed Tantawi.

The meeting had the backing of both the President of the Palestinian Authority and the Prime Minister of Israel; with security, there were forty people in the delegation. Nothing could have prepared us for what was to come. Intense discussions took place, but the original document was now proving to be a stumbling block for part of the delegation. The Archbishop of Canterbury described chairing the round-the-clock negotiations as the hardest of his life, but at the end of the second day we finally had the agreement of all parties, and the Alexandria Declaration was signed. For the first time in history, all the faith traditions of Israel and Palestine had come together to call for a religiously sanctioned ceasefire and an end to violence.

However, this historic day and historic document were not ends in themselves, but the beginning of an equally complex process. This process would take place against a background of increased violence in the land they call Holy, including a major backlash against the Palestinian Authority by Israel, called Operation Defensive Shield. The parties to the declaration took a role in the negotiations to end the siege of the Church of the Nativity of Bethlehem and various other conflicts that had a significant religious dimension. Part of the agreement called for a permanent committee to implement the declaration, and it has since met regularly to try and move forward what became known as the Alexandria process.

Eventually out of the Alexandria process has come the religious track of the Middle East peace process. This track recognises the need to engage with both religious and political leaders. It has never sought to replace the political process but to complement it, working with politicians to try and implement a lasting peace in the region. The process is complex and has involved the establishment of various centres in both Israel and Palestine that seek to make known the religious dimensions needed in peace-making.

Despite offers of funding from the G8 and the Palestinian Authority, the process has chosen to accept financial support from the United States Institute of Peace, the British and American governments, Coventry Cathedral and the Church of Norway. It is a very expensive process always lacking in resources, but it is a continuing work and it is evolving all the time. Since the declaration was signed, new initiatives have been developed to address concerns about women, education, humanitarian aid, social reform and education.

It was at a meeting in Europe that a member of the audience asked one of our leading sheikhs, Tal el-Sadr, how he saw his role. After listening to the question he took Rabbi Melchior's hand and said: 'Rabbi Melchior is my brother and we will walk this long and difficult road together until we find peace, for my job is to pull up the thorns on the road and to plant flowers.' Sheikh Tal el-Sadr was one of the founders of Hamas and now he is totally dedicated to the search for peace.

The belief that people can change is fundamental to the search for peace; if people cannot change then there is no point in this work. Peace will never be found by nice people talking to nice people; on the whole it is not the nice people who cause wars. Our challenge is to engage with some of those who are responsible for the perpetuation of violence, or if not those themselves, those who can influence them.

As Professor Hans Küng has said: 'If there is no peace among religions there will be no peace among nations.' Since 9/11 we have become acutely aware of the level of danger in the world, and it is imperative that religious leaders are involved in peace-making in the Middle East and elsewhere. Already the Alexandria Declaration has inspired peace-making in other parts of the world where there is conflict, not least in northern Nigeria and Iraq. There is no easy solution or magical answer to religious peace-making. It is long-term and difficult work, and requires people who are committed to the issue for years to come and not just today. That is why the partnership with the United States Institute of Peace is so important, as this is one of the few agencies that recognises both the lengthy nature of the work and its difficulties. A great deal of time is spent in the region each month simply encouraging the different partners to keep at this search for peace, or else trying to gain permits for the Palestinian delegates to enter Israel for key meetings.

It is engaging with 'the other' that breaks down the demonisation that has kept the parties apart. Opposition to our work comes from many different sources, not least the religious leaders themselves. Then there is political opposition or even diplomatic opposition, which often comes when leaders in these areas feel threatened because we are doing work that either they are meant to do or have failed to do. At the same time it is often these very people who have provided immense support, who have been secure enough in themselves to work with us rather than against us.

Searching for peace in post-war Iraq is a very different matter and one that was never going to be easy with such an ethnically and religiously diverse nation. Early contacts with both the British Foreign Office and the US State Department revealed that religion and religious peace-making were not high on the agenda of either. One letter from the Foreign Office stated that the priority had to be getting water and electricity functioning again. At this stage it was only the United States Institute of Peace and various private individuals who saw the need for religious peace-making in post-war Iraq. Within days of that Foreign Office letter we received a message from the British government that sorting out water and electricity was proving impossible because religious and tribal issues were getting in the way.

Early on it was decided that the Ministry of Awqaf (religious affairs) was problematic and thus would not be established in the initial transitional government (the Coalition Provisional Authority, or CPA), and many within the CPA were greatly distressed by this. There were indeed problems with the former ministry, but this was true for all the pre-existing ministries. Relationships with the Iraqi religious leaders could not be formed overnight, and it was therefore highly fortunate that for the previous five years I had been working closely with many of Iraq's religious leaders, the good and the not so good. These relationships proved to be vital after the fighting had stopped.

Of specific importance was our relationship with Ayatollah Hossain al-Sader, and it was with him that many of our early, crucial meetings took place. On several occasions I was asked by the American ambassador, Paul Bremer, to arrange a meeting for him with the ayatollah. Having been a persecuted Shia majority leader, the ayatollah now had prominence in the new Iraq, and at an early post-war meeting he stated that an institute for religious tolerance was needed. In-depth discussions began as we tried to work out how this vision could become reality. Building on the Alexandria Declaration in Israel and Palestine, it was decided that a meeting of the key religious leaders should be organised, at which a document outlining the plans could be signed.

Days were spent visiting the various religious leaders to gain their support for the initiative. While most of them were very positive, many were extremely difficult. Some leaders were convinced that I was really a CIA agent trying to get them to admit guilt for the developing insurgency. It was when they realised that I was a close friend of some of the Sunni leaders who were very prominent before the war that their attitude towards me changed. With the realisation that the Sunni minority was feeling increasingly marginalised, it became one of our early priorities to try and encourage Sunni leaders to play an active role in the restoration of Iraq. However, many were afraid that if they were seen working with us they would become a target for violence, and sadly this proved to be true. The day after we had taken a group of Sunni leaders to meet with members of the CPA, the home of a sheikh who had been working alongside a key Sunni figure for a year was bombed.

Meanwhile work continued on the foundation document for our institute of religious tolerance. A meeting was arranged for 23 February 2004, at the Babylon Hotel in Baghdad, and the British government agreed to pick up the bill. Chaired by Dr Mowaffak al-Rubaie, a Shia member of the Governing Council, it attracted a wide variety of religious and tribal leaders, and debate was intense. The group was concerned about the prospect of their nation falling into sectarian divide. Eventually the document was signed and the meeting ended with the pledge to establish a Centre for Dialogue, Reconciliation and Peace.

Over the following months work intensified, while at the same time the religious tensions between the various communities grew. The main division continued to be between Shia and Sunni, and this was exacerbated by the ongoing 'de-Baathification' process, which was seen by many as being a means of targeting the Sunni leadership. Many of the Sunni tribal and religious leaders had their assets and money sequestrated and had to leave Iraq because they could no longer afford the security that they now needed.

The signing of the document that became known as the Baghdad Religious Accord was just the beginning of the process. What was to follow was an increasingly complex process of continued inter-religious dialogue. This was not the nice inter-faith encounter that is often experienced in the West; it was, and continues to be, inter-religious dialogue at the cutting edge. It is often painful, there is shouting and tears, but in the end there is usually greater understanding and a renewed commitment to the search for peace.

The centre formed as a result of the signing of the Baghdad Religious Accord eventually became known as the Iraqi Institute of Peace. It was found outstanding premises in Baghdad, but even this was not without its problems, as each religious group wanted it in their own area. On the evening of its opening, in the Shia area, it was surrounded by thirty-nine armed guards protecting the various dignitaries inside. Not the usual setting for the opening of a centre for peace, but this was Baghdad, one of the most dangerous cities in the world.

Immediately the IIP set about establishing various forums to oversee its main objectives. The Women's Forum, for example, examines how women fit into the new Iraq and in particular the role of religious women. Following its launch, which had the support of clerics from all parts of the religious spectrum, the first items on its agenda were to work towards an end to domestic violence and to reform the law that allows for multiple wives.

The Forum for Inter-Religious Dialogue focused on the need to create an environment whereby this new phenomenon could take place. In the old Iraq there was an unnatural respect of 'the other' based on fear rather than understanding, and there was little if any real dialogue and encounter. The IIP is building genuine understanding and respect between people whose views are different.

The role of the media in Iraq today is not without controversy. Every form of media has its own political stance and this can be particularly problematic when you are trying to establish an environment of peace in the midst of chaos. The IIP's Media Forum has sought to enable the present media to understand the significant role they can play in creating an environment where peace can return, producing its own written materials to enable the message of peace to be heard.

The Youth and Young People's Forum aims to ensure that the message of tolerance, understanding and peace-making is adopted by the next generation. We all know that young people are the future, but trying to influence them positively is not always easy. The IIP works with and challenges the Ministry of Education, schools and youth institutions, as well as religious leaders, about the way they relate to young people.

The Conflict Resolution Forum has by necessity been one of the most active, seeking not only to deal with different aspects of the ongoing conflict but to work for the release of the many hostages that have been taken since April 2004. Since the hostage crisis began, the forum has successfully assisted in the release of several individuals. Many more have been killed, and it is particularly hard on the staff of the organisation when they seemingly fail at the task in hand. Recently one of our own staff was killed while searching for a hostage. However, the many disappointments have not prevented the team from continuing their crucial work.

The final forum deals with the issue of human rights and religious tolerance. This has been a key pillar of Iraqi reconstruction, partly because there were such grave human rights abuses under the former Iraqi regime. There is now a government Ministry for Human Rights, but once again the religious dimensions of this enormous subject had been forgotten. Like all of the IIP's work it was clear that this was not just a Baghdad issue, so centres have been established throughout the nation. The aim of this forum is to learn from the mistakes of the past, and not to bury them but to use them to help people and the nation move forward.

The challenge to create a peace respected by religious and secular leaders has been huge. Winning the war is easy compared with gaining the peace. Iraq teaches us that it takes as many resources to make peace as to wage war, or rebuild the country after the conflict. As yet they are not available, although the United States Institute of Peace and the British Foreign Office have provided a huge amount of support in terms of funds and training.

Religion can and must play a crucial role in peace-making, not just in the Middle East but throughout the world. We need our government to take it more seriously so that it is not just seen as a sideline to peace-keeping but one of the core issues. The reality is that governments to date have been scared of religion and its role in conflict. They have avoided it, as if to pretend that these issues will go away if they are not confronted. They will not; they will continue to increase. On 9/11 the world changed, and the root of that change was not just sociological and political, at its heart it was religious.

In the last Conservative Party manifesto I was delighted to see that there was a pledge to provide an ambassador for religious freedom. This is very much needed, but of even greater importance is the need for an ambassador for religion and conflict, or should I say religion and peace-making. In America there is at least a congressionally funded Institute of Peace. It was created at the same time as the US Center for Strategic Studies, an organisation that balances somewhat the billions that are spent on war. I am not a pacifist, we need a good strategic defence policy, but we also need to deal with the religious components of conflict if we are to aspire to a world that is safe.

In closing I want to stress that if faith is going to play a positive rather than just a destructive role, we must ensure that the international community resources religious peace-making, and that bodies such as the Council of Christians and Jews and the newer Three Faiths Forum have the funds necessary to do their work.

Clifford Hill, in his book *The Wilberforce Connection*, states that a 'fully comprehensive inter-faith dialogue ... is essential for the future peace of the world if we are to be saved from a century of religious violence that threatens to engulf the whole world'. We need to ensure that we do not live in a world where those of different faiths demonise each other. In the words of William Wilberforce:

> How can we judge fairly of the characters and merits of men, of the wisdom or folly of actions unless we have ... an accurate knowledge of all particulars so that we may live as it were in the times, and among the persons of whom we read; see with their eyes and reason and decide on their premises?

2006

Caroline Spelman

In the spirit of Wilberforce as a reformer, I have chosen to talk to you about regeneration – the rebuilding of lives, not just places. I believe community regeneration is one of the most serious issues facing any postmodern government, and tonight I want to focus on what makes for successful regeneration and finally some, although by no means all, of the practical measures I think we need to take.

For decades governments of different political persuasions have been trying to regenerate deprived parts of this country. This regeneration has taken place under a seemingly endless variety of initiatives: 'Urban Aid', 'Enterprise Zones', 'City Challenge', 'Going for Growth', 'New Deal for Communities', 'Sustainable Communities', to name but a few. I think you'd agree that where there has been a failure in regeneration policy over the decades it has not been for want of a catchy slogan.

Yet as a recent Joseph Rowntree Foundation report shows, most of the wards that were deprived a century ago are still deprived today. When I was first elected to my constituency I asked how it was that after millions of pounds of the single regeneration budget fund had been spent on an estate, its four wards still counted among the bottom 10 per cent most deprived wards in the country, with eight years' lower life expectancy than the rest of my constituency.

I just want to restate, if I may, that in those areas of deprivation, life expectancy was nearly a decade less than elsewhere. For those of us who believe in the sanctity of life, that is a horrifying statistic and one which is unjustifiable in the modern age. The further injustice is that this disparity is increasing as we all live longer.

This pattern is replicated when it comes to general poor health. Research carried out in the 2001 census found that self-reported ill health stood at 20 per cent for the unemployed or those having never worked, as opposed to just 5 per cent for those in managerial or professional employment.

As well as poor health, my three most deprived wards suffer double the national average rate of unemployment and very poor levels of educational attainment. You have to conclude that a lot of what has been done is not working. The purpose of my lecture tonight is to examine why this is and what we need to do differently.

Cynics might say why bother, but only the most hard hearted can suppress the desire to help when we see others in need. A Christian has an absolute duty to help. From the earliest books of the Bible we read: 'There will always be poor people among you. Therefore I command you to be open handed towards your brothers and towards the poor and needy in your land' (Deuteronomy 15.11). More starkly, on the Day of Judgment Jesus warns us that we will be held to account for our failure to feed the hungry, clothe the naked, care for the sick and visit the imprisoned (Matthew 25.32). Nor is neglect of the needs of the poor an option politically. Our deprived communities are just that – ours – and we are all in this together, trying to work out how to help. That is what David Cameron means when he talks about shared responsibility. We cannot hide behind the fact that we are the world's fourth largest economy when the fact is that many people here live in Third World conditions. I do not believe we will be returned to power until we demonstrate our willingness to engage with the needs of our most deprived communities, most of which are urban.

For me, and so many others who are involved in this issue, regeneration is essential if we are to improve the places where people spend their lives, and it is an issue where the spiritual and political imperatives meet. There is a powerful legacy in our political history of trying to give people a hand up out of poverty. From the slum clearance initiative of Disraeli, through the regeneration schemes of Chamberlain, to the rehousing programmes of Macmillan, improving the living conditions of the poor in society has been a traditional strength for us and one that we need to reclaim as our own.

That is why we are launching a month-long campaign on regeneration starting in Liverpool next week, with the whole shadow cabinet on the case. It is significant that we are returning to Liverpool, for it was here that Michael Heseltine founded a successful City Challenge project. This was a bold regeneration initiative from which, twenty-five years on, we can learn useful lessons. But while the rebuilding of Albert Dock and London Docklands achieved long-lasting improvements for local people, other City Challenge projects – in Bethnal Green and Tipton in the West Midlands – were less successful, and it is important to face up to why. I have looked though 140 regeneration projects and one key message to emerge is that if regeneration is something we do *with* the community it is more likely to succeed than if it is something we do *to* a community. If the community is involved, listened to, engaged with, and ultimately takes ownership of the changes it wants to achieve, it is more likely to succeed. Take the City Challenge project in Castle Vale, Birmingham. The Vale, as it was known, had a bad name: a 1960s Radburn estate with unpopular high-rise blocks of flats, high-density housing, few amenities and synonymous with crime. By the use of a housing action trust run by residents for residents, the tower blocks were brought down and a mix of owner-occupied and rental homes introduced in their place. New amenities were built, such as a Sainsbury's and a state of the art primary care centre, which has halted the rate of infant mortality.

What Castle Vale demonstrates is that regeneration is not just about buildings and the environment but also about people. A deprived community often suffers from a very low level of self-esteem, and this brings me onto the first objective of regeneration, which I see as being the rebuilding of civic pride.

It may amuse you to learn that since taking on this role I am a frequent visitor to what used to be the old red-light district of Birmingham, a place called Balsall Heath, about which we shall hear more a little later. The way in which it has been turned around is best illustrated in the words of one of its residents, who said to me recently: 'We used to feel embarrassed to say that we live here, but we don't any more.'

This is because residents have cleared out the prostitutes and cleaned up the streets, making this one of the safest wards in Birmingham. That new civic pride is the key to the regeneration of a community. People need to feel good about where they live and have a shared sense of responsibility in making it that stay that way.

If you visit northern industrial towns you will be struck very often by the grandeur of their town halls and civic buildings. These magnificent constructions were demonstrations of civic pride and became beacons for the local community. In a sense the buildings were a visual representation of the community spirit that existed, and likewise many of the decaying and derelict properties that characterise areas of deprivation visually represent a decay of civic pride and community spirit. When people feel uplifted about where they live it is just one part of a whole chain of circumstances that improve people's quality of life. But it's hard to feel uplifted when your street is scarred with graffiti, the pavement is littered with beer cans and the nearest green space is a no-go area. Turning that around takes a combined effort and needs the support and contribution of the whole community.

However, this needs nurturing and it needs driving, and at the heart of that is the role of a 'local champion', who can bring people together and channel their efforts. Sometimes termed a 'capacity builder', this is somebody who can identify other individuals, groups and resources that can help deliver change at a local level.

The key to regeneration is to find a local champion who can inspire and lead their neighbours in a campaign that achieves and sustains change, in the way the community wants. They may be mums and dads who want their children to grow up on cleaner, safer streets, or a local teacher who sees how the school provides a hub for a community, or a local pastor – as with the Baptist minister on my estate who runs a carers service from within his church. Such people are not easy to find in communities that are conditioned into having things done to them, and which are mistrustful of authorities that decide what they think is best but then change their mind or never come up with the goods. They are especially suspicious of politicians of all persuasions. So we need to build the confidence and skills of the local champions we find.

The regeneration then becomes personal. I have seen lives transformed by involvement in community renewal. Mums on the Sure Start programme with very low self-esteem learn that they are good at raising their children and go on to provide learning support in schools, and now some that I know are taking degrees to become teachers. They will be the best possible role models for the children in their care. Dads who were out of work learn alongside their children in schools where the IT suite is open after hours to help make up for an education that failed the parent. Dad wants to learn how to read so he can follow what his own child learns.

And there are those presently not part of the community who

can share in this process of renewal, such as the homeless, the drug abusing and the imprisoned.

What is so often the common denominator in deprived areas is the loss of control people experience over their lives. Be it through homelessness, substance abuse or actual imprisonment, people feel no longer in a position to take responsibility for their own lives, and we need to help them rebalance the situation so that they gradually take more and more control back. I firmly believe people grow into their responsibilities, but that does not negate the need to help them grow.

John Bird, editor of the *Big Issue*, is a living example of individual renewal now giving new life to the community. Once homeless, now leading this successful charity, he points out that just putting a roof over someone's head is not enough – they need the work to pay for it. So buy a copy of the *Big Issue* next time you see it in the knowledge you are helping rebuild a life. In that small gesture of buying a magazine from that street vendor you are actually illustrating the culture that we need to foster for successful regeneration, the culture of encouraging and helping someone to take control and help themselves and others.

Let me give you another example. A charity I chair, called Welcome, helps drug abusers get a job and hold it down, and we have many ex-offenders among our clients. These people are released from prison without anywhere to live, rarely a job and sometimes neither clothes nor money. Small wonder reoffending rates are so high. Far from being restorative, our justice system seems antediluvian.

I can feel you thinking: Caroline, what does it cost? I have resisted the temptation to talk about money because all too often Conservatives seem to be talking about tax and public spending. I want to confront this head on by saying that I do not believe that our reflex should always be how will this affect the rate of tax. There are certain things it is worth paying extra for because they serve the common good.

That said, regeneration is actually one of the few examples where by deploying amazingly little money you can see massive rewards, rewards that not only improve the lives of residents immeasurably, but that also enrich society as a whole.

Down the years millions have been wasted in regeneration projects that have not worked. If I tell you there are presently fifty different funding streams for regeneration you will see that there certainly isn't efficient use of resources. Funding is often time limited. How many projects do you know which have a grant for only three years? This stems from the political habit of announcing eye-catching initiatives as if the announcement itself would fix the problem. What we don't do well is appraise and sustain those that are a success.

Too often regeneration is seen as only physical. If I was to ask you what springs to mind if you think about an area that has been successfully regenerated, I imagine more often than not you think of graffiti being removed, gardens and green spaces being improved, perhaps smart new street furniture.

Of course these things are a vital part of any successful regeneration project but I think we can fall into the trap of thinking that the physical improvement of a neighbourhood is an end in itself, when in fact the sustained physical improvement of a neighbourhood actually follows on from the personal regeneration of the lives of the people living there.

In short, not enough attention is given to the human element of regeneration. In many cases a sense of community needs to be built and nurtured. Often when we talk about deprived communities, the sad reality is that the sense of community diminished long ago and what is left is fragmented associations of individuals co-existing. We need only look at our city suburbs to see that the vacuum left by communities is soon filled by the culture of gangs and territories.

This shouldn't be surprising. For young people who feel socially disaffected, gangs provide the comfort and security and kinship that would in days gone by have been offered through being part of a close neighbourhood community. They fill the need held by many for a sense of belonging and a sense of identification with where they live.

If regeneration is to be successful it has to foster and sustain neighbourhoods and communities and provide a shared identity that supplants the culture of gangs and gives people an alternative, broader and more prosperous sense of association.

We need to replace the culture of 'What's in it for me?' with a new sense of 'Good for me, good for my neighbour'. But community cohesion is a Delphic sort of thing. The difficulty from my point of view, from the view of any politician, is that you cannot deliver that from central government, you cannot craft legislation to provide for it and you cannot simply allocate funds to deliver it. It has to grow from the grass-roots up.

But politicians can help create a framework for community cohesion to flourish. We can start by acknowledging and building on the proud history that many communities have, by offering opportunities and resources that will unite local people rather than divide them. It is about giving the whole community ownership of the projects and a stake in its success.

This can't be done through the wholesale demolition of houses as proposed in the Pathfinders scheme; it is lunacy to think that tearing down the physical structure of a community will heal the social divisions within it. I feel passionately about this issue and I see Pathfinders as cultural vandalism writ large. It is the equivalent of saying to those communities: 'You are beyond salvation so we will level you to the ground and start again'. Is that really the best we can do?

How can you expect people to regain a sense of civic pride when the government is effectively giving those areas a sense of shame? If you go to Liverpool, East Yorkshire, Teesside or any of these places you will hear this view from local communities. The tragedy of Pathfinders is that it is doing the opposite of what history shows us needs to be done for successful regeneration. It is concentrating on buildings instead of people; it is being done against the wishes of local people and with no involvement from them. It is being imposed on them from above, and it is destroying any sense of community cohesion that previously existed.

We need to make sure that government delivers the climate, opportunities and, yes, the resources, to enable people to reclaim the places where they live and regenerate the lives of the people around them.

Education is at the heart of regenerating a community that suffers from low self-esteem and a culture of under-achievement. Parents instinctively want the best for their children and that instinct can be harnessed to help raise the aspirations of the whole community. The school is often one of the only amenities on some of our soulless 1960s housing estates, and each school has its community of mums and dads, nans and grandpas, willing the next generation on. The potential to regenerate these schools as centres of life-long learning is huge. If the state education system failed you it can be hard to cross the threshold again. So let's be creative here: two portals, one for adults and one for children. Schools can provide training and advice in and out of regular hours for those in and out of work. It is a tremendous resource in a deprived community, but it needs to be open at a time when people can access it.

It is only through education, be it academic or vocational, early learning or adult learning, that people can be empowered to make choices and take control, but delivering that education remains a challenge in areas of deprivation. The Office for National Statistics report *Focus on Social Inequalities*, published in August 2005, found that the profile of children who are most likely to be low education achievers is: male; from a low socio-economic background; with parents who have no or low qualifications; living in a single-parent household; having many siblings; attending a state school with a high rate of free school meal eligibility. But even where educational attainment is improved, this gives rise to a second challenge, the challenge of developing communities and neighbourhoods which manage to retain an educated population rather than simply equipping them to move on and move out.

This is where the role of job opportunities and security come in. Historically residential settlements have developed around centres of employment for local people, be it the shipyards along the River Tyne, the farms of the Sussex Weald or the manufacturing industry of the West Midlands. The era of long-term, population-sustaining mass employers has passed and as a country we have had to embrace the move to more short-term, flexible and often service-based industries. This transition has left many communities in limbo, existing without the economic rationale on which they were founded.

This process was articulated by a town planner called David Higdon, who was asked about the decline of Newcastle's West End. He said: 'In the forty-year cycle (1945–85), first the workers were rehoused but then their traditional jobs, the reason for being there, were removed. It amounts to a planning non-sequitur.' Yet at the same time you have other parts of the country, in some cases other parts of the same city, positively overheating with demand for business and living space.

I passionately believe that we need to find more effective ways of balancing economic growth more evenly across the country. My team is undertaking a piece of research entitled 'Exploring the Barriers to Economic Growth' and it has the remit of looking at how we can spread what I would call the London effect up through the rest of the country. Of course, you would expect that of me, I am a West Midlands MP and I share the slightly chippy feeling that prevails north of the Watford Gap that everything in the UK seems to revolve around London. But it is a startling fact that the world's tenth largest economy is London and the south-east, with other areas not benefiting from this; they are at best lying fallow, at worst fostering an underclass of the future.

In 1845 Benjamin Disraeli spoke of 'two nations; between whom there is no intercourse and no sympathy; who are as ignorant of each other's habits, thoughts, and feelings, as if they were dwellers in different zones, or inhabitants of different planets'. More than a century later there are still parts of the country where this analysis holds true.

What I hope my research will do is identify the obstacles to creating a better economic balance and provide a blueprint for overcoming it. I anticipate this will include everything from transport links and crime levels, through to the availability of a skilled workforce. But I see every reason to be optimistic that the advancement of IT and new working practices will be instrumental in delivering greater economic growth. Jobs and employment opportunities are increasingly portable and we need to seize this as a vehicle for delivering more balanced economic growth.

However, as I implied, it is not just about economic balance between parts of the country, it is about economic balance in many cases within the same town or city. Many central business districts have been rebuilt, but around them languishes a collar of decline as people move out to the leafy suburbs and green fields beyond, then commute to the 'grey deserts' to work. This is not sustainable, and our next big idea needs to be a new model for attractive near-city living.

The reasons for people's flight from the suburbs are various, but factors such as levels of crime, performance of schools and quality of the local environment all contribute to whether or not a neighbourhood is one that people want to move into and live in. The problem is that these issues are self-perpetuating. As soon as an area gets a reputation as somewhere that you wouldn't want to bring up a family, then families stop moving into the area and so it quickly goes into decline – a decline that is obviously made more difficult to arrest once it is well under way.

Helping people and communities to help themselves is for me the very essence of being in politics. The reality is, you can't tell people to get on their bike if they have never been shown how to ride it, and I see the role of government as being like a pair of stabilisers, running alongside communities until they are able to go it alone.

We need to devolve real power down to local councils so that they can properly respond to the needs of their communities. Local government is best placed to see what needs to be done and to relate to local people, and we are missing a massive opportunity by denuding it of powers and turning it into a mere agent of Whitehall.

We need to draw in the expertise of the voluntary sector, which already has a proven track record of delivering local solutions. Instead of government trying to constrain these organisations, it should be trusting them and giving them more opportunities. We need to harness the spirit of social enterprise and run with it, lauding flagship examples such as Balsall Heath, Castle Vale and the smaller-scale credit unions, foyers for homeless people and individual learning plans for disadvantaged children.

Commercial enterprise has become the bedrock of our economy, and so social enterprise can become the bedrock of our communities if we are brave enough to let it. It's a gamble for politicians as we rescind a great deal of responsibility while being held accountable at the end of the day – I can understand the caution over that, but the gains it can offer are plentiful.

David Cameron

First I want to do something quite simple and straightforward, which is to acknowledge the pain and devastation that slavery has caused, and which the legacy of slavery still causes, to Africans and to people of African origin across the world. In the history of humankind, the slave trade stands out as one of the greatest crimes ever committed by man against his brother. The reduction of a human being to the status of an economic unit, to be bought and sold for his utility to another man, represents an absolute denial of the dignity and equality of every individual.

Slavery has existed since the first civilisations appeared on earth, but the transatlantic slave trade is rightly seen as the eternal symbol of slavery. It was systematic, organised and authorised by the law of the most powerful nation on earth: Britain. It is almost impossible to imagine the suffering involved.

People were captured in their villages and fields. They were force-marched to the coast and held in dungeons, then they were consigned to the holds of ships where they spent weeks or even months at sea. As a contemporary witness records, men and women were 'chained two by two, right leg and left leg, right hand and left hand. Each slave had less room than a man in a coffin.'

In these dark, cramped, airless conditions diseases spread quickly. The dead were left to lie among the living and if a slave protested or rebelled, he was simply thrown overboard, his manacles dragging him to his death. On one occasion in 1781, aboard the slave ship *Zong*, more than a hundred slaves were thrown overboard to stop the spread of sickness and protect the owners' investment in their human cargo.

Over many years, this vile trade was a staple industry of the British Empire and it is estimated that up to twelve million men, women and children were sold into slavery in the Americas. A large proportion of them were sold under the British Empire – captured for a market controlled by British businessmen and taken to plantations owned by British settlers.

So let me acknowledge the pain and the legacy of slavery today in the words that William Wilberforce himself used, in his first speech moving the abolition of slavery in 1789: 'I mean not to accuse anyone but to take the shame upon myself, in common indeed with the whole Parliament of Great Britain, for having [allowed] this horrid trade to be carried on under their authority.'

Let me make it clear that I, and the Conservative Party, do not give all the credit for abolition to one man. William Wilberforce was the leader of the parliamentary campaign, but beside him stood some dozens of activists and campaigners. As he wrote to the Prime Minister when the Abolition Act was passed in 1807: 'I am only one among many fellow labourers.' These fellow labourers were not all British, they were not all men, and they were not all white.

I think of Hannah More and Margaret Middleton – female campaigners who inspired the parliamentary campaign – but of course it wasn't just high society that resisted slavery. By the end of the eighteenth century, thanks to the efforts of a lady in Leicester called Elizabeth Heyrick, hundreds of thousands of households were boycotting West Indian sugar – a mass movement led by women.

I think also of the black campaigners, such as the writer Equiano and the freedom fighter Sam Sharpe. Black writers today point out that one of the most pernicious legacies of slavery is the sense of shame that millions of people allowed themselves to be enslaved. Well, they didn't – most resisted, actively or passively, and some stand as heroes for oppressed people everywhere. Young black people can find role models in the history of the abolition movement.

And yet it is right that, this year at least, we remember William Wilberforce. To me, he is an eternal example of what passion and commitment and integrity can achieve in politics.

Wilberforce represented to his generation and to the world a radically different idea of what politics is for. In his day most politicians stood, first and foremost, for sectional class interests, and beyond that they represented the exclusive interests of the nation. At the international level, foreign policy was about the practice of statecraft, detached from questions of morality. More than any other politician, William Wilberforce changed that.

He elevated the role of the politician to something nobler than the defender of sectional or national interests, and he convinced his country that there was something higher than statecraft – the pursuit of moral goals and the betterment of mankind. Most important of all, Wilberforce helped turn the vast power of the British Empire to moral purposes.

Overall, I believe that the contribution Britain made to America, Australia, India, the Far East and southern Africa in the Victorian era was a good one. The institutions of law, banking and government, which Britain exported to her colonies, are among the greatest benefits that one nation has ever given to the world. But in nothing did Britain earn her right to be the most powerful nation on earth more than in this, that in the second half of the nineteenth century one of the primary tasks of the Royal Navy was to stamp out slavery on the high seas.

As John Stuart Mill put it at the time: 'For the last half-century [the British] have spent annual sums equal to the revenue of a small kingdom in blockading the Africa coast, for a cause in which we not only had no interest, but which was contrary to our pecuniary interest.'

So let us have a balanced understanding of the Empire and Commonwealth. It is to Britain's eternal shame that we supported the slave trade, but it is to Britain's eternal pride that we stamped it out. Both of these things need to be known and remembered by our children.

I want to finish by addressing the future, because today we are not only remembering the slavery of the past but bringing to mind the many thousands of people who are still trapped in slavery, trafficked as labourers, sex workers and soldiers in the developing world or here in the West. Between 700,000 and two million women and children are trafficked across international borders every year.

The dedication of William Wilberforce and his colleagues is still needed today, and I salute the efforts of modern campaigners to end this vicious abuse of human rights. We must also address the state of Africa today. I am pleased that there is a political consensus in Britain on the need for debt relief and foreign aid, and I want my party to lead the debate on how we can help Africa beyond this.

Wilberforce himself, in that first speech in 1789, said this: 'Let us make reparation to Africa, so far as we can, by establishing trade upon true commercial principles.' We should be doing all we can to promote indigenous economic development, and this means reducing trade tariffs and helping African nations develop the institutions of economic growth.

There is a golden thread that links property rights, free markets, free trade, the rule of law, honest government, sound finances, economic progress and social advance. I want that to be the great project of this century, comparable with the role Britain played in stopping slavery 150 years ago. And here at home, there is something else I want my party to do – to help bring about the proper representation of black men and women in our national life.

It is not political correctness to want Parliament and local government to mirror the nation it represents, it is a simple recognition of the need for role models in all walks of life. I want children of every background and community to be able to look at the institutions that lead our nation – the judges' bench, the armed forces and, yes, Parliament itself – and see adults there that they can identify with. To be able to say 'If I work hard, I can get to the top'.

As leader of the Conservative Party I must play my part in this. In the past, my party has failed to recruit MPs and local councillors who reflect the ethnic diversity of our nation. As I hope you have heard, we are seeking to change this, and we are making progress. We now have three times as many black and minority ethnic candidates as we have MPs, but that's not enough. We must do more, and I hope you will help.

The best legacy of this anniversary would be for today's black children to say in the future: 'The anniversary changed things. That was the time my mother or my father decided to stand for election.' So don't think of politics as someone else's business, think of it as your business. Think about standing. Think about taking part. Think about making your voice heard in the councils of our nation.

Finally, let me thank the Conservative Christian Fellowship for putting this celebration together today. It is natural that it was Christian campaigners who led the fight against slavery in the British Empire, and it is right that it is Christian churches that are today leading the commemoration of the abolition of slavery. In the words of Isaiah, the Messiah came 'to proclaim freedom for the captives'.

I salute the work of you and your predecessors in fighting for freedom from slavery around the world. Politicians are often accused of not being the best of listeners, but I had the pleasure of listening to a short address by Pastor Nims Obunge at the church service at our party conference in Bournemouth last year. It was rather like my wedding day, as the sermon seemed to be addressed just at me. Pastor Nims told me: 'The problem is that politicians are too concerned about the next general election. We need statesman who are concerned about the next generation.' Amen to that.

As we gather to remember William Wilberforce and his fellow labourers, let us work together to build on their achievement. Let us stand together to fight racism and exploitation in the next generation. Let us work for the betterment of our country and the world.

James Jones

In spite of, or maybe because of, the attention that has been given to the bicentennial anniversary of the abolition of the transatlantic slave trade, I sense that many in our society are still wondering what all the fuss is about.

Much of my own ministry has been in Bristol, Hull and Liverpool, and my own diocese is united with Virginia in America and Akure in Nigeria, in a partnership that replicates the slave trade triangle. The people and places have opened up my imagination to the realities of racism so inextricably chained to trade in black slaves. Slavery, in one form or another, has always been and remains, even to this day, a feature of human society. The International Labour Organization estimates that 179 million people are caught up in forced labour, that 218 million children between five and seventeen are engaged in some form of slave labour, and 2.4 million are victims of sexual trafficking. What was distinctive about the transatlantic slave trade was its overt racism. The millions of slaves were African and black.

Recently I was part of a consultation on the environment in America that took place on an old cotton plantation in south Georgia. We were addressed by a black pastor from Atlanta who had been with Martin Luther King on the steps of the Lincoln Memorial when he had given his celebrated 'I have a dream' speech. The pastor said, only half jokingly, that he'd felt nervous coming to the plantation, especially when he'd seen the Old Oak Tree. The mainly white gathering froze in guilty embarrassment. The hanging of black people because of the colour of their skin was for him and his audience within their living memory. The roots of racism cannot be disentangled from the history of slavery. Racism is the legacy of the transatlantic trade.

Those who wonder what all the fuss is about fail to see this connection and underestimate the destructive power of racism in the modern world. In Liverpool we came face to face with its ugly manifestation when the young, talented and black Anthony Walker was murdered with an axe in a hideously brutal racist attack. The taunting and bullying of a person because of the colour of his skin has its antecedents in the dehumanising treatment of black people who were traded in their millions from Africa to America in the vilest of barbaric conditions and in ships that sailed out of London, Bristol and Liverpool. I can barely bear to tell you this but one such slave ship was actually and cruelly named *The Blessing*. Estimates vary, but at least ten million slaves were transported and at least one million died in transit. Did I say 'died'? I should have said 'killed', because the mode in which they were traded was grotesque and deliberate. The remarkable autobiography of Olaudah Equiano called (and this must be a classic example of English understatement) *An Interesting Narrative* catalogues the brutality of the life at sea and testifies to the tragic lot of the slave in transit.

> The stench of the hold . . . became absolutely pestilential. The closeness of the place, the heat of the climate, added to the number in the ship, which was so crowded that each had scarcely room to turn himself, almost suffocated us. This produced copious perspirations, so that the air soon became unfit for respiration, from a variety of loathsome smells, and brought on a sickness among the

slaves, of which many died . . . This wretched situation was again aggravated by the galling of chains . . . the filth of the necessary tubs [latrine buckets], into which the children often fell, and were almost suffocated. The shrieks of the women, and the groans of the dying, rendered the whole a scene of horror almost inconceivable.

For those who survived, the conditions on arrival were equally harsh. On a visit to Virginia I was taken by a young black priest to stand on the banks of the James River where half a million slaves were traded in Richmond. She showed me Lumpkins Jail, where they were corralled before being sold, and the gallows where they were hanged if they rebelled. I wept for the shame of it. I think I wept also out of a sense of mystery, for here I was in the presence of a young black woman who had embraced the faith of the very people who had been her ancestors' oppressors. I was standing on the same soil as grace. It brought into sharp focus the relationship between Christianity and the trade in slaves.

The fact that William Wilberforce became a committed Christian and championed the passing through Parliament of the bill to abolish the slave trade could be, and indeed has been, taken by Christians to be both evidence and example of how Christianity inspires radical social action and transformation. Although that is an attractive thesis and has within it seeds of truth, the fuller picture is much more complicated.

As Christopher Leslie Brown in his book *Moral Capital* has shown, the relationship between Christianity and slavery and its trade was sadly more ambivalent than that. The Establishment countenanced both slavery and the trade, fearing that abolition would threaten the British Empire with economic ruin. The bishops, with the notable exception of the Bishop of Chester, Beilby Porteus, who later went on to become Bishop of London, sided with the Establishment. Adam Hochschild in his book *Bury the Chains* tells of a plantation in the West

Indies which was owned by the Society for the Propagation of the Gospel in Foreign Parts, whose governing board included the Regius Professors of Divinity at Oxford and Cambridge and the Archbishop of Canterbury. The estate's brand, burned onto the chests of slaves with a red-hot iron, was SOCIETY. The clerics on the society's board noticed the plantation's high death rate, but made no move to change how it operated. 'I have long wondered & lamented', wrote the Archbishop of Canterbury to a fellow bishop in 1760, 'that the Negroes in our plantations decrease, & new supplies become necessary continually. Surely this proceeds from Defect, both of Humanity, & even of good policy. But we must take things as they are at present.' So much for the prophetic moral vision of the Church of England.

Even the Evangelicals, who eventually emerged as a driving force of the abolition movement, were possessed of a personal piety which sought principally the conversion of others so that slave-owning converts in the colonies would lead more upright lives and their converted slaves would become more industrious.

Brown and other historians show that there were many factors at work in the complex history of the abolition movement. This brief lecture does not offer space to debate these so I simply note some of the forces at work in the world that contributed to the context: the American War of Independence, the war with France, the changing shape of the British Empire, the philosophy of liberty emerging in Britain, the Quaker movement, the Evangelical revival and in the colonies the growing and courageous resistance of the slaves themselves. All these played a part in the changing social context but, as always happens, there appeared on the stage of this new world significant players whose lives and actions would not only increase the drama but seemingly change the course of history: Thomas Clarkson, Hannah More, James Ramsay, Margaret Middleton, Olaudah Equiano, John Newton, William Wilberforce to name but some. Each merits a biography, let alone a lecture.

John Newton exercised great influence over Wilberforce. Newton had commanded a slave ship and led a troubled and dissolute life. Shipwrecked and in fear of death he converted to Christ. In spite of his spiritual awakening he continued to command a slave ship, which again poses questions about the relationship between slavery and Christianity. Indeed his testimony of his Evangelical conversion is full of repentance, yet not about how he treated black slaves but rather about blaspheming. When he fell ill he became surveyor of the tides in Liverpool before then becoming a priest and prolific writer of hymns, including 'Amazing Grace how sweet the sound that saved a wretch like me'. He acted as a mentor to Wilberforce, whom he met first as a boy of twelve, and was the only slave ship captain to give evidence of the 'heinous evil' to the Parliamentary Commission on the Slave Trade. But it took Newton some thirty years from his conversion to speak out publicly against it, as he himself acknowledged: 'During the time I was engaged in the slave trade, I never had the least scruple as to its lawfulness, I was upon the whole satisfied with it, as the appointment providence had marked out for me ... It is indeed accounted a genteel employment, and is usually very profitable.'

Yet it was through the likes of Newton that Wilberforce sensed that following his own Evangelical conversion his future lay in applying Christian principles to public policy. As Brown and others have shown, this was not familiar territory for Evangelicals, whose puritan emphasis was on personal salvation and individual piety. What was it that propelled the Evangelicals out of their subculture and into the public arena so that for at least half a century they became the driving force of social reform in nineteenth-century Britain? It's a lesson Evangelicals seem to have to learn afresh in every generation because the Evangelical tradition often pulls in a very other-worldly direction.

John Coffey of the Jubilee Centre offers a detailed analysis, but at the risk of oversimplifying I want to identify three key features about the Evangelical contribution to the abolition movement and the social reform agenda.

First, William Wilberforce personified in himself the connection between public affairs and private faith. Here was a figure who was immersed in public life not least through his membership of Parliament and his friendship with William Pitt, the Prime Minister. He was also immersed in Evangelical spirituality through his conversion and fellowship with the Teston group and the Clapham Sect. Here was a man baptised in both public affairs and private faith, in personal salvation and social action. And others would later follow, most notably Lord Shaftesbury.

Secondly, Evangelical Christianity takes you back to the text of the Gospels and has the potential to subvert what is known as 'nominal Christianity'. Wilberforce himself wrote a book entitled *A Practical View of the Prevailing Religious System of Professed Christians in the Higher and Middle Classes of this Country Contrasted with Real Christianity*. How's that for a snappy title?

Evangelicalism differentiates itself from formal religion by emphasising the need for a personal response to Christ and demonstrable change. It was distinctive, and it found in the abolition movement an opportunity to express its spiritual and moral distinctiveness. In Wilberforce it found a leader and provided him with a following.

Thirdly, the changing social and political context provided a new forum in which to debate and to explore the meaning of the ancient text of Scripture. The Bible is a dynamic book. In different times and cultures its themes and principles will variously come to the fore, just as in this period Christians are discovering in the Bible hitherto unemphasised texts about the earth and our environment. In the late eighteenth and nineteenth centuries, Christians – and especially Evangelicals, who attach to scripture a primary authority – were discovering serious and vital principles about the brotherhood of humanity, deliverance and liberty, loving your neighbour, guilt and judgement, repentance and atonement and jubilee.

All this was informed by and informed the general debate about slavery and the trade, culminating in the Abolition of the Slave Trade Act of 1807, which came about through an alliance of people, both black and white, who not only responded to events with spiritual wisdom but also challenged the prevailing view with moral courage.

On a personal note I am honoured to give this brief contribution to the Wilberforce Lecture in this bicentennial year. Ever since I was a student I have been inspired by William Wilberforce and the example he gave of applying to public policy the values of the Kingdom of God. He took forward the conversation between the world and the Word, and in concert with others helped change the moral landscape of the empire through the abolition of the transatlantic slave trade and eventually slavery itself. They brought closer a vision of the human family which Christ himself saw and acted upon.

I would like to end with an episode from the life of Christ which challenges the racism that is the legacy of the transatlantic slave trade: the Cleansing of the Temple. It is true that most commentators have interpreted this as a statement by Christ against commercialism, but such an interpretation falls short of its full meaning and obscures a crucial element in the story. The significance of what Jesus does is found in his quotations from the Old Testament and in realising where in the temple the action took place. The stalls were set up in the Court of the Gentiles, the place where the other races could draw near to the God of Abraham and Moses. By filling the court with market stalls the authorities were denying the other races their sacred space. Jesus overturned the tables quoting from Isaiah and Jeremiah, and insisted that the temple should be 'a house of prayer for all races'. Over the years we have neglected this emphasis, preferring instead to concentrate on the 'den of thieves'. We have failed to see the true nature of the robbery. What was stolen was the vision of every single race being able to worship God together in His house of prayer. The cleansing of the temple was as much an action against racism as it was against unbridled commercialism. In Isaiah, from which Jesus quotes, the prophet holds before us a vision of God's Kingdom where people of every race within the human family come together, joyfully, to worship God in all his glory. It's a vision to die for. Many have, and Jesus did. It's a vision, a dream that has yet to come true.

If, as I believe, racism is the legacy of the transatlantic slave trade, then even 200 years on we are heirs of this evil. We need moral and political leadership that not only names the prejudice but also acts in a just and merciful way to embrace every ethnic group in contemporary Britain, where the Christian faith has shaped the law, liberty, language and the landscape of our nation. In this respect we need a new generation of men and women like Olaudah Equiano and William Wilberforce.

Katei Kirby

In the year that we mark the bicentenary of the abolition of the slave trade, I made my first visit to an African country. Malawi, which is known as the warm heart of Africa, welcomed me in a way that I found deeply connecting and deeply disturbing at the same time. Connecting, because of the similarities in food, body language and expression, and my instant adaptation to the warmer climate. Disturbing, because in between the natural beauty and pockets of prosperity were clear signs of acute poverty and deprivation. It was in talking to local people, and hearing their concerns and aspirations for their country and its people, that it became clear that some of those visible signs of deprivation had their roots in a particular mindset that had been handed down through generations, resulting in a legacy for some of poverty, a legacy that the government and churches are working to address.

In preparing to speak to you this evening I came across a range of books, articles, official and unofficial websites, blogs and podcasts, dedicated to exploring the impact of the slave trade. While each author and contributor had given a distinctive emphasis, tone and focus to the information, none left me in any doubt as to what slavery was – and indeed is.

Across the range of information, two common threads emerged. The first is that the footprints of the deplorable and systematic enslavement of human beings have been left across every country, continent and culture. Where enforced, slavery devalues human life without exception, and people become property. Where endorsed, slavery is seen as a measure of economic strength or a means of political persuasion. The second, and perhaps the more challenging, thread is the role that the church and the Christian community played in both the advancement and the abolition of slavery. What is clear is that both threads have left legacies.

A legacy is defined as 'a bequest made in a will, something from the past, and something outdated or discontinued'. And so 200 years after the British Parliament said 'no' to the slave trade, it is important to ask ourselves what has been bequeathed or left from the past. What has been inherited and by whom? The legacies of the slave trade are many and could keep a research fellow occupied for a considerable time, so I have grouped the legacies of slavery into three areas: the pains of the past, the problems of the present and the potential of the prophetic (or the future).

Dr Joy DeGruy-Leary says that 'we must return and claim our past in order to move toward our future'. Many who have traced their history and heritage have found that looking back means acknowledging events and information that are painful to process, and in some cases, difficult to disseminate. Coming face to face with the knowledge that your ancestors were either robbed of their identity, value and dignity, or that they were perpetrators of these atrocities, opens up a plethora of challenging emotions and experiences that some have found difficult to process, while others have been confident enough to channel them into something beneficial. The question we each need to ask ourselves is: what in our history contributed to the pains of the past?

The second broad group of legacies are issues that manifest themselves in superior or inferior behaviour within or between people groups. These problems of the present include disrespect for human life, disregard for authority, disparagement of identity and, in a growing number of cases, disdain of belief and faith.

Slavery blurred, and indeed in many cases destroyed, lines of heritage and lineage for those people groups whom it was forced upon, deconstructing what many believe to be the foundation of a stable community and society – the family. This process is still occurring today.

Slavery displaced Africans across the Americas, the Caribbean and Europe, and despite abolition, the aftermath of slavery continues in various expressions of segregation, inequality and racism. Individual and institutional racism has been cited as the catalyst in a myriad of violent and often criminal actions that have made the headlines locally, nationally and internationally. Martin Luther King said that 11 a.m. on a Sunday morning is the most segregated hour in America, a statement that still seems to ring true here in the multicultural UK.

Gaps in educational achievement indicate the continuing disparity of access in learning, and the over-representation of black people in mental health institutions and the criminal justice system clearly reveals the mindset towards those considered less able because of their background and heritage. The question we each need to ask ourselves is: what in our history contributes to the problems of the present?

Before, during and since abolition, many voices have championed the cause of the marginalised, the disenfranchised and the displaced. In the eighteenth century, Olaudah Equiano was among those who spoke and wrote about the possibilities that a 'free' future could hold for his people and all people. In the twentieth century it was Martin Luther King who spoke and wrote prophetically about the future, raising the hopes and aspirations of millions of African Americans. Later in the same century, Nelson Mandela could be heard championing the cause of the oppressed in the fight against apartheid in South Africa.

These three and others were bold enough to speak in their time, for their time and for the future, but not without risk or cost. The legacy that they have left was and is prophetic. The question we each need to ask ourselves is: what in our history contributes to the potential of the prophetic?

To date, we have heard from those who have expressed regret for the slave trade. Those expressions, although welcomed by some, were perceived by some as hollow because of the absence of an act of regret. We have also heard the calls for reparation, which, if carried out like a refund from a high-street store with a no-quibble policy, will simply reduce the rich and priceless heritage of the people, their personalities and potential ravaged by slavery to a monetary value.

In my view, an apology or expression of regret is insufficient if done in isolation, and there is no cheque that could be written to repair or replace valuable lives that were tragically and brutally lost because of slavery. A lasting legacy would be an act of repentance and reconciliation – a visible and tangible act through which our churches, communities, agencies, businesses and governments demonstrate a lasting commitment to the reality of abolition by investing in the present and future of those disenfranchised by the negative legacies of the slave trade.

The footprints left by slavery cannot be ignored or forgotten. On the contrary, this painful and problematic era of our history needs to be told and retold, accurately, so that history is the right story. I call on Africans and Caribbeans to record our story, acknowledging our part in the slave trade and the legacies it has left. In doing this, I believe that we will not only learn from the mistakes of the past, but play our part in leaving a legacy of knowledge that will better serve those who have risen out of slavery. It will also ensure that legacies that currently appear negative can be appropriately recognised and better understood.

Martin Luther King said: 'I have a dream.' I say, I have an expectation: an expectation that one day the legacies we rehearse about the slave trade will lead to the legacies of abolition, which include an honest recognition of the pain of the past, a willingness to address the problems of the present, and a strong desire to see the potential of the prophetic. I also believe that if we want to be, each of us can be part of the answer to Jesus's prayer for unity in John 17:21, and play our part in the restoration of identity, of value and of dignity to human life right across every custom, culture, country and continent.

2008

Dominic Grieve

When I learnt that the suggested topic for this evening's address was 'Britishness', my political antennae quivered a fair bit at the prospect of a minefield. Even defining the concept is fraught with danger – many have had a stab, and many have failed. But it is a responsibility of politicians to address difficult subjects. Quite apart from anything else, we are engaged in promoting Britishness. We ought therefore to be able to justify what it is we are trying both to be part of and to celebrate.

While we find it hard to define exactly what Britishness is, we are still attached to abstract symbols that represent nationhood; the British, or Union, flag in particular. When Kelly Holmes won gold at the Olympic Games in Athens, every newspaper carried a photograph of her wrapped in the Union flag. When British troops won victory in the Falkland Islands, they carried with them a Union flag. When crowds thronged The Mall to celebrate the Queen's Golden Jubilee, many were waving Union flags.

These people carried their flag with them in their moment of triumph because, I suggest, their sense of achievement was made complete by associating themselves with not just a personal success but one for their community – their country. They are British, they are proud to be British, proud to associate themselves with being British, and proud to be contributing to being British. This archetypal symbol of unity added to and expressed their sense of self-worth.

In contrast, too often we hear about unfavourable displays of Britishness. The British disease in the 1960s was a byword for careless, expensive and uncommitted workers. More recently, anything that is seen as unfavourable or undesirable tends to earn the same epithet. Put the phrase 'British disease' into Google and out come references to alcoholism, gambling, yobs and even bad teeth. Indeed, anyone who has been in Prague on a Saturday night will have seen displays of behaviour by British men, in particular, which could not be described as edifying.

That there is now confusion about Britishness is without doubt. Part of the confusion comes from muddling different concepts. 'Britishness' is an identity that has an emotional charge, whereas British citizenship is chiefly seen as a portal to the consumption of state services, with little requirement to subscribe to a common identity as such. These two ideas have clashed. In contrast, my father, in the early twentieth century, was brought up in an environment where British identity and citizenship were assumed to be inextricably linked. Travellers did not even require a passport. This relied, of course, on stereotypes, but it was no less powerful for it. As writers on national identity such as Amartya Sen have shown, imagination and shared emotion play a key role in minimising difference and creating, at best, a comfortable and sustaining environment for all sections of society, from which my father and his contemporaries benefited.

In recent years, despair that there is little collective sense of national identity has set in for some. As a member of Parliament I receive several letters a week from constituents telling me that they can no longer identify with the country that they are living in. These range from older people, who say that they are planning to go and live in Spain or France, to younger ones who indicate that they are intending to emigrate, usually to the United States, Australia or New Zealand. In virtually every case the moving force does not seem to be economic. Rather, it seems that their emotional attachment to this country has disappeared. It's like the breakdown of a personal relationship.

Some bemoan the loss of 'traditional British' values. Others talk darkly about immigration and feeling they are foreigners in their own land. But what is clear is that they feel robbed of what they thought was common property. They believe that they will have more freedom to maintain their old values and be able to express their British identity better in Torremolinos, the Dordogne, Sydney or Ohio.

Yet others have welcomed change.

For a long time there has been a consistent pattern of those on the political left attacking national symbols and culture for anti-establishment reasons. They argue that these reinforce traditions and hierarchy and are thus inimical to socialist progress in creating a new society. They have sought to deconstruct our culture. But as their efforts were resisted by the innate conservatism of the population, the preferred weapon has been the imperative need to adapt Britishness to diversity by multiculturalism.

The former mayor of London, Mr Livingstone, has been a supreme champion of multiculturalism. He devoted a large budget to encouraging compartmentalised self-expression in each ethnic or religious grouping under his patronage. The justification was that each were victims of discrimination and required support to assert themselves.

Such a policy subtly creates inimical divisions: minority groups such as Jews do not want to be treated as minorities, and resisted the patronage offered; majority groups such as white working-class young males, whose attitudes are held to require change, also resisted.

Under Labour, multiculturalism has further infected Whitehall departments – although much of it started long before in municipal government. For example, government directives from the former Department of Education have insisted on the relevance of any distinctive national history being played down. The Department of Communities and Local Government provides grants based on racial and religious groupings rather than general objective tests of need.

Don't misunderstand me, the presence in Britain of people of many cultures is an enriching fact. In our age of global population movement it is vital that we understand and respect the contribution and value that other cultures can bring us. I believe that familiarity with diversity can add to our national wellbeing, a larger pool of talent encourages creativity and broader comprehension of the human condition.

But most immigrants arrive here with the culture of their country of origin and, usually, little knowledge of our own. Instead of the state taking active steps to help harmonisation, under the creed of multiculturalism the opposite has happened, because new arrivals have been encouraged to think of themselves as different from those already settled.

The result is that, in too many cases, the children or grandchildren of the original immigrants appear not to have come to terms with the culture of the country in which their family are now living. I have been chilled to discover at meetings with young educated Muslims the level of alienation from the society that has nurtured them through its state education system, and the anger with it that some of them show. A few so dislike their fellow citizens that they are quite happy to kill to achieve their ideological end of an entirely different kind of society, based on the re-creation of an imagined seventh-century civilisation, their concept of which owes far more to myth than to reality.

Trevor Phillips, once chairman of the Commission for Racial Equality and now chairman of the Equality and Human Rights Commission, has summed up the effect of multiculturalism as 'sleepwalking into segregation'. He saw, as many are now realising, that multiculturalism endangers societal cohesion, as it emphasises group rights over national collective wellbeing.

We then witnessed experiments in trying to substitute a brand new national character. Remember the Cool Britannia project? This was a politically motivated plan to rebrand our national identity that found its best expression in the Dome – that supreme white elephant. As avoidance of anything traditional at the millennium was de rigueur, it ended up pretty dull. It did not work any more than did the experiment to 'globalise' the British Airways livery. It is interesting to contrast this with the Carnaby Street era of the 1960s, when British symbols – from the flag to the policeman's helmet – were hijacked naughtily and with wit to promote creative new ideas. The humour then played on the underlying importance of the national symbols represented.

The disaffection felt by many Britons clearly shows that neither new synthetic symbols, nor multiculturalism, have provided adequate compensation for what is felt to have been lost.

This isn't surprising. While Labour governments and left-leaning commentators have earnestly emphasised the contribution of other nations and cultures to our polity, the one group that has received a disproportionate amount of opprobrium is the English. The English make up 85 per cent of the population and are a vital ingredient of the British mix.

Margaret Hodges's recent attack on the Last Night of the Proms serves to highlight the problem. She said she disliked this vibrant cultural event, which gives enjoyment to a large number of people, because it was not inclusive enough. She was far from clear what it was that she wanted included that would remedy this deficiency. The National Eisteddfod in Wales, which one might reasonably argue is much more exclusive, was not attacked. Nor is the custom of my Punjabi constituents to dance to bhangra music (as I did last week) in celebrating Vaisakhi. The Eisteddfod is seen as an important cultural manifestation of being Welsh, bhangra and Vaisakhi of being Punjabi. The Last Night of the Proms is, with its folk songs, sea shanties and patriotic hymns, quintessentially English. That is what seems to have upset her.

The relentless undermining of English national consciousness has been marked. English heroes and heroines, from King Alfred and Henry V through Nelson, Florence Nightingale, John Wesley, Shaftesbury and Lawrence of Arabia, are largely forgotten. Children are left with vast areas of ignorance as to how their country has been shaped by the contributions of their forebears. In contrast, it remains fashionable to celebrate other heroes, such as Scotland's William Wallace – star of an historically inaccurate film epic.

Even William Wilberforce was, until last year, a peripheral figure in our national consciousness outside of academic and some political or religious groups. His re-emergence has been partial. His role in the abolition of the slave trade is of course of worldwide significance, but it was his zeal for the reformation of manners, grounded on his religious beliefs, that lay at its heart. That is a subject likely to make modern progressives rather less comfortable, but it certainly helped shape the next 150 years of British social history.

I also noted with amusement that recently Martin Kettle, an apologist for New Labour, attacked Gordon Brown for the simplicity of his nationalism. Noting a St George's flag hoisted above Downing Street on St George's Day he wrote in the *Guardian*:

There is much more to creating a cohesive society than putting out more flags . . . the potent English traditions that have nothing to do with flags and everything to do with the tradition of Shakespeare, Bunyan, Blake, Shelley, Morris and Orwell – of a free, shared and inspired England that has never existed but remains, in the Albion of our imagination, the England many of us desire.

I could not agree more. But the trouble is, who knows of this aspect of the vision today?

It is in stark contrast to the experience in other European countries. By the time I finished my French state infant schooling in London, I had been provided with an overview of France's 'story' replete with key figures from the cavemen to de Gaulle, of which I can still recite large chunks. It is still the same today.

The English have also lost out on political governance. The British state in its old constitutional form was the English state adapted to encompass the diversity of new participants. But that is a different thing to what we now have after devolution. There is a widespread perception that England is now disadvantaged and disempowered by new national institutions that give special privileges to all except the English. It is this as much as the narrower West Lothian question that produces problems. Lord Irvine argued that these would go away if we stopped thinking about them. But you can't stop people thinking.

We should not be surprised, then, that British identity has decayed, as the English contribution has always been its single biggest component by virtue of population, language and history. Dual identity is, and has always been, at the root of the British state. The Scots, the Welsh and the Irish, who have not suffered the same cultural neglect as have the English, appear to be more comfortable with their own identity and better able to celebrate it than the English. Polling research shows that by 2003 a sense of equal dual identity had declined to 41 per cent of English, 23 per cent of Scots and 29 per cent of the Welsh. If dual identity cannot be maintained in old established relationships, there is no pattern to inspire newcomers to our country, or for them to aspire to.

Where there is a void of this kind it is inevitably filled by something else, and this has happened with unfortunate consequences. Where a new breed of citizen was intended, freed of the shackles and constraints of the past and, therefore, more accepting of radical ideas and difference, we have instead Englishness as yob culture. History is littered with ersatz national cultures produced to fill the gap where cultural continuity is repressed or broken: Russia at the end of the Soviet period and Germany in the 1930s spring to mind. As an unconscious understanding of time and place, and one's own position in it, disappear, so self-confidence erodes and, with it, the ability to welcome, understand and tolerate difference. It creates the politics of cultural despair – the recruiting ground of groups such as the BNP and Hizb ut-Tahrir.

I see this when meeting people, and particularly younger people, of all backgrounds, from recent immigrant to long-established white British. They tell me they do not believe that they live in a society that has any defining ethos at all and have no concern for Britain save at best as an environment for the pursuit of narrow self-interest. When it is suggested to them that they live in a country where there are shared values that can enhance their quality of life, they are uncertain what these are. Responsibility for the collective wellbeing of the country may lie with others but not with them.

I suggest that this is where it has all gone wrong for New Labour. As they are finding, it is easier to abandon, destroy and negate than it is to create. There is a frenzy of activity to redefine and reinvent Britishness in an attempt to pull people together again. We have seen numerous constitutional proposals by the government and, indeed, the possibility of a Bill of Rights and Obligations. We have also seen many attempts to define citizenship, culminating in Lord Goldsmith's report *Citizenship: Our Common Bond*, with some interesting ideas among others much less good. We now know that Gordon Brown vetoed the idea of a national song, but there is still the national motto – the best suggestion for which I have heard was 'Mustn't grumble'.

The problem with all this effort is that, however worthy, it's artificial, as was made so clear by the hostility to Lord Goldsmith's suggestion of having citizenship ceremonies for all eighteen-year-olds. There was no resonance with its target audience.

The government is again equating state citizenship with Britishness. People cannot be told to be British, they have to feel that they are British. Being British is to accept as part of one's identity the legacy of shared past endeavour, to celebrate the present benefits of Britain and to look with hope to a shared future. From it comes a willingness to accept the constraints that allow that future to emerge through the democratic process.

People can be told that they are citizens and that by being so they have certain rights and civic responsibilities, symbolised by being given a passport or an ID card. However, it is what the 'citizens' then do and think which has and will create a national culture – it is this way round.

A national culture, externalised as a national character, is organic – it is emotionally charged, a theatre in the round enacted every day in our national institutions. For too long the majority have been told their values and institutions are unworthy. Forty years of political correctness and the socialist denigration of the past have left people with little to hang on to. By denigrating the essential ingredients that constitute a national character, such as institutions, traditions, ceremonies and history, Labour has removed the architecture of Britishness. The result is that we have lost confidence in what has made us British. While that loss of confidence lasts, no amount of state invention will adequately substitute for it. Loss of a shared sense of Britishness is not a cause but a symptom of the real problem.

So I return to the question posed to me: Britishness – useful or redundant? Should we, and can we, restore a sense of Britishness?

I believe that the things which unite us in common bond and can bring us together and command respect are still there, but they are hidden beneath the surface. Let me illustrate what I mean. Today Scottishness is heavily underpinned by cultural manifestations based on a 'Gaelic' identity. In fact, most of Scotland has never spoken Gaelic and the tartan kilt, modern bagpipe and cult of Scottishness has few links to the culture of the country as it existed before the eighteenth century. It was, as Hugh Trevor-Roper revealed in his essay 'The Highland Tradition of Scotland', an invention of the nineteenth century. But so what? There is no doubt that its success was due to the new identity going with the grain of public feeling. The Scots were seeking to produce a rope from the strands of their past to guide them, a sense of time, place and belonging in a period of great change during the industrial revolution, and they succeeded. What rope of collective identity can we now twist which might go with the grain?

Whether it is PC or not to say, within the Union, historically, the English have made the foremost contribution to our British political values. It was not for nothing that Lord Palmerston in his famous 1850 statement Civis Britannicus Sum said: 'So also a British subject in what ever land he may be shall feel confident that the watchful eye and strong arm of England will protect him against injustice and wrong.'

He knew where the strength came from. It's the thing most often raised with me by immigrants as a reason for coming here. The fundamental English contribution to Britishness lies in our law and in our freedom under it. From the Saxon moot court and Magna Carta through the Glorious Revolution of 1688 and onwards, freedom under the law has been central to what English, and with it British, national identity is all about. During the course of the eighteenth century and thereafter, our national identity was built around the concept of limited government. In the eighteenth century, as Ben Wilson so graphically illustrates in his book *The Age of Cant*, there was a willingness to tolerate considerable levels of anarchy and disorder in the belief that any attempt at remedying it would remove freedom at the same time. Only the English could put the slogan 'Wilkes for

Liberty' on a teapot. We exported these principles to America where they remain vibrant – some think too vibrant!

But freedom under the law is being eroded. In the past ten years we have seen willingness by government to bypass basic legal principles in the name of administrative efficiency and control. The proposed power to detain a suspect for up to six weeks without charge, control orders, a plethora of criminal justice legislation, trying to remove judicial review in asylum cases, the attempts at various times to limit trial by jury and to change the burden of proof in some criminal cases to facilitate conviction, all highlight this transformation.

We have also seen the rise in administrative penalties without trial, be they ASBOs or fixed penalties, and the arrival of intrusive powers to acquire and retain national databases detailing information on the law-abiding. The law is also now dominated by trivia, and too much time is devoted to regulating minor matters.

These are all things that bear the hallmarks of tyranny. Some of them were prohibited in those ancient laws such as the Bill of Rights 1689, Habeas Corpus in 1679 and the Five Knights Case of 1628. As someone who is half-French, I now find myself astonished that there appear to be increasingly fewer safeguards in this country for individual freedoms than in France, something that I would never have considered possible thirty years ago. Indeed, with the absence of a written constitution, the abandonment of unwritten conventions on the way the state operates in relation to the citizen is easy. We are a conventional nation. It's just not done. Abandoning convention you abandon the nation.

The proffered justification for all this is, of course, that it makes our lives safer and softer. Yet the evidence for this is not present. On the contrary, the changes in the relations between individuals and the state leave the former feeling utterly disempowered. They thus start to depend on the state for problem-solving to an extent that is impossible for the state to fulfil. The inevitable demoralisation and irritation with authority does nothing to make people feel confident in a state that promises what it can't deliver. It undermines all notion of individual responsibility and neighbourliness.

Freedom under law requires freedom of thought and expression. Our country has defined itself for many generations as a place where freedom of expression – philosophical and religious – could be practised and, indeed, the whole trend in our history for 200 years is the gradual removal of the fetters of censorship on people's views and, to a great extent, their behaviour, subject to the protection of others under our criminal law.

But now forces are pulling in the opposite direction. We are being told that the price of diversity must be restrictions on freedom. As we saw with the Incitement to Religious Hatred Bill and later, with the Equality Act legislation and the Sexual Orientation Regulations debate which followed from it, the trend is now to restrict freedom of thought, expression and the rights of individual conscience in the hope of achieving a greater equality and tolerance of difference across our country. A street preacher in my constituency was told by the police that he could preach the Gospel, but that it was harassment to warn people that they might go to hell if they did not repent.

This runs entirely counter to what England's historical experience of living with divergent ethical, political and religious views has given to Britishness. The development of our country into a liberal democracy was not achieved through repression, although it was at times tried. It came principally through the growth of tolerance based on Christian principles and their interplay with Classical Greek humanism. Anglican Christianity, in particular, is as defining of the English character as it has been important to developing Britishness.

First, as the Archbishop of York so rightly said in his recent Easter sermon: 'Our identity as a nation owes more to our Christian heritage than many care to admit.' Writing in the eighth century, the

Venerable Bede, 'the father of English history', wrote not only of how the English were converted, but how the Gospel played a major socialising and civilising role in this country, by uniting the English from a group of warring tribes and conferring nationhood upon them.

Secondly, the Reformation initiated a diversity of viewpoints that moved us from religious uniformity to pluralism. This came about through a process of polemic, debate, argument and, occasionally, violence and terror. Gradually we achieved a state where the tolerance of the beliefs of others was seen as better for our collective wellbeing than imposed solutions and persecution. The Vicar of Bray may have been a figure of fun, but his ability to accommodate himself and the willingness of different regimes to let him accommodate himself may be viewed as one of the more benevolent contributions to our culture. This didn't happen in Wales, Scotland or Ireland until much more recently. The tolerance of Protestant dissenters in the late seventeenth century, Catholic emancipation in 1829 and Jewish emancipation in the 1840s are key moments in the process, and each has unlocked the possibility for different groups to participate in the public and political sphere from which we have all benefited. It is not for nothing that there are English pubs called the Live and Let Live.

As a result, our forebears were able to release a torrent of good works, through institutions, for the benefit of the wider community, that are nowadays seen as being one of the key characteristics of Britishness. Our society is underpinned by independent voluntary participation, religious and secular, from faith schools, charitable foundations for the relief of poverty, hospitals and Barnados to the RNLI.

To return to that excellent Easter sermon of the Archbishop of York:

Whilst it is, of course, true to say that such virtues as kindness to neighbours, fair play and common decency are not unique to the

Christian faith, just as they are not unique to Britain, it is equally true to say that these virtues have become embedded in our social fabric and heritage as a result of the Christian faith and influence on society.

I must emphasise here that I am not about to advocate trying to turn the clock back to some rose-tinted past. You cannot turn clocks back, and roses fade. The nature of our society has changed recently with startling rapidity. An era of population churn and greater diversity must be recognised. But it seems to me that the zealous regulation of our conduct and belief, whether moral or religious, the imposition of state-defined orthodoxy on public and private attitudes, and the overburdening of law and regulation, with objectives that are unattainable, have the unintended consequence of undermining the chances of creating better cohesion in our country. It is through constant contact and exchange of views that we moderate each other's attitudes and behaviour. By this process, my practice of Anglicanism, although recognisably traditional, is nevertheless distinctly different from that practised by my sixteenth-century forebears. The same can be said of the Islam practised by Ismaili Muslims, prompted into dialogue and involvement in Western public life by the Aga Khan. Similarly, my political beliefs as a Conservative, although clearly in a philosophical tradition that can be traced back to the eighteenth century, are very different in practice from the politics of that era, as a result of being moderated by the impact of socialist and other systems of thought that have arisen since.

I, therefore, suggest that one of the key problems we are facing at the moment is that state-imposed norms are inducing a sclerosis in the exchanges between individuals and groups that is preventing the organic development and renewal of British national identity. Whether narrow nationalist or religious fundamentalist, the opportunity has never been better for those who wish to argue that the compartmentalisation of one's existence into comfort zones with a narrow appeal is better than toleration and co-operation with others to achieve common goals.

If we want a common British identity – and I believe we need one – then I would recommend the first thing we must do as politicians is to let go a bit. If individuals and families are freed from the constraints of regulation and the dictates of political correctness to find their own relationships with each other, then the common themes that form any national culture and identity will emerge of themselves. We already know that, within two or three generations, immigrants' descendants take on the accent of the area in which they live. In a dynamic society, the same exchange that leads to a common voice will express a community of values as well.

We can, in government, also take steps to facilitate this evolutionary process. First, as Trevor Phillips has recognised, a cohesive nation state with shared values will be difficult to achieve as long as immigration is not limited to a rate that allows for integration to occur as a natural process. It is perfectly obvious from the level of discontent engendered that current levels are unsustainable. Rates of immigration are a matter on which existing citizens have a legitimate right to have a determining view. Attending to the views expressed by British citizens of every ethnic background is an essential step in promoting cohesion.

Secondly, we need to imbue citizenship with more status than it has at present. Its acquisition should not be seen as a consumer good but as a privilege that carries with it clear responsibilities to others. Both main parties are feeling their way to a possible Bill of Rights that also may enshrine responsibilities. But if these are to be effective they need to be taught as civics in schools in the context of a good understanding of our history.

Suppression of, and damage to, English national identity must be addressed. It is a question of restoring balance to the Union, not of encouraging an English separatist agenda. Given devolution, we must deal speedily with the West Lothian question and provide England with better control of its affairs.

We need to restore the principles of freedom and equality under the law as central to our nationhood. Just as Britishness is being undermined by perceived inequalities in the treatment of the different constituent groupings of the UK, so it is also by a system of governance that gives privileges to particular ethnic and religious groups and not on the basis of need. Celebrating our heritage of freedom under the law means maintaining it for tomorrow and reversing the trends that are disempowering the individual against the state.

If we do these things then I think it is likely that the community of values we seek to create will coalesce round those things that people naturally share in common. Britain, for all its shortcomings, remains attractive as a place to make a life for oneself and one's family. That some groups fail to settle is more likely to be the result of stifling the process by which individuals influence each other's behaviour than by the inherent characteristics of any particular group. If, therefore, we give them that opportunity, the re-creation of shared national identity will happen naturally. It will not, of course, be the same Britishness as in the 1940s. For that matter, Britishness in the 1940s was clearly very different from Britishness in the 1720s or in the 1850s. But the Britishness of the 1940s was no less British for being different from that of earlier periods.

If we can set the right political conditions, then we will acquire a national identity that is vibrant, rooted in our past history, resilient and flexible in accommodating newcomers. That will be as useful to us as the abstract process currently being carried out by New Labour to reinvent Britishness is redundant.

2009

Ken Costa

In Westminster Abbey there is a statue to commemorate the life and work of Wilberforce. It bears a lengthy inscription that includes these words: 'In an age and country fertile in great and good men, he was among the foremost of those who fixed the character of their time.' I would argue, 200 years later, there is no more pressing imperative than to fix the character of our time. Our finances are broke, our moral fabric is threadbare, our political system beleaguered and our society broken. We almost cry out for change.

Britain has experienced two quite extraordinary national crises: the first financial, and the second political. Our entire financial system has come closer to the brink of collapse than at any time in living memory, closer than anyone would have imagined possible. Then we have seen a political crisis, with the revelations of MPs expense claims drastically damaging public trust in our political system, which was already dangerously low.

At the same time, we have a social crisis as we see the cohesion of our society being torn apart. We claim rights, but personal responsibility for our actions is all but disappearing. So knife crime, crimes against the person, teenage pregnancy, binge drinking, family breakdown and attacks on children shock us with every new revelation. No longer can we apply the word 'community' to vast tracts of our urban society, where even the memory of the reality of being together and supporting each other has disappeared.

Our current financial and political crises offer us the opportunity to assess our priorities afresh. Indeed, we have a unique opportunity for our generation to fix the moral and social character of our time. It is my belief that divorcing economics from the moral and spiritual dimensions of life has been the single most important contributor to the most severe financial crisis in living memory, the collapse of trust in politics, the breakdown of our social structure and the pervasive lack of purpose in life felt by individuals across the country. All of these, at root, are about how we have silenced what I call 'the moral spirit'.

Wilberforce was a man of famously wide-ranging interests. The Westminster Abbey inscription to him describes how he was born in Hull on 24 August 1759 and died in London on 29 July 1833, and how he was 'a member of the House of Commons for nearly half a century'. It also tells how 'his name will ever be specially identified with his exertions to abolish the African Slave Trade and how he endured great obloquy and great opposition' for his campaign. But the slave trade was not his only passion. Shortly after his conversion Wilberforce wrote in his journal that 'God Almighty has set before me two great objects, the suppression of the Slave Trade and the Reformation of Manners [what we would call moral values]'.

Following the bicentenary of the abolition of the transatlantic slave trade, marked by books and films such as *Amazing Grace*, Wilberforce's anti-slavery campaign has become well known, and we rightly celebrate his role in suppression of the slave trade. But we need also to recover the second of his life's callings – the reformation of the moral condition of the nation. This is the neglected part of Wilberforce's legacy.

In many ways Wilberforce's countrymen faced similar issues to our own. Bishop Berkeley said that the moral and spiritual degeneracy had reached a degree that was never before known in any Christian country: gin was destroying the social fabric of society; crime, general lawlessness and gambling had become national obsessions; one in ten people in London lived off criminal, illegal or immoral earnings; the national economic condition was shaky; financial fraud was rife; immorality was almost a sport; pornography sold well and daylight fornication was just one of those things. The country had lost its way. It was in need of profound personal and social reform. Sir William Blackstone, after visiting the churches of every clergyman in London, said: 'I did not hear a single discourse which had more Christianity in it than the writings of Cicero. It was impossible to tell from a typical sermon whether the preacher was a follower of Confucius, Muhammad or Jesus Christ.'

Wilberforce himself lived the high life while at university, but then his life turned. He found a living faith and his life was changed. As William Hague, in his biography of Wilberforce, points out: 'Now and for the rest of his life, religion was never to make Wilberforce dreary, melancholy or intolerant.' He goes on to say that Wilberforce objected to those who would

> render Christianity so much a system of prohibitions, rather than of privilege and hopes, [among whom] the injunction to rejoice so strongly enforced in the New Testament is practically neglected and religion is made to wear a forbidding and gloomy air, and not one of peace, and hope and joy.

William Hague rightly observes that this was 'an attitude which meant that he was never shunned socially or politically, but could combine what had always been an appealing personality with a force of steadfast belief'. His genius was to remain human and accessible to all. The key objective of his life 'would always centre on using spiritual improvement to ameliorate the human condition by practical steps . . . he thus sought a higher moral climate for the betterment of rich and poor, law-abiding and law-breaking alike'.

As we all know, it is dangerously easy for those burning with a cause to appear almost inhuman in their obsessions; distant from the very people they are trying to help, people who end up being more put off by their zeal than persuaded by their convictions. It was a deep work of the spirit of God that enabled Wilberforce to combine a colossal sense of calling together with a natural happy manner and interest in people.

In this, as in so many other things, we can learn from Wilberforce. He was no Bible basher. His skill was in persuasion, in presenting arguments to support his cause, in mobilising and organising, in effectively lobbying not only the masses but the movers and shakers of the age. The key themes of his life were justice, faith and the wellbeing of others. Above all he believed that to accomplish the personal and social changes needed in England, the whole heart of every individual needed to be engaged. Only then would the regeneration of society follow. He knew that one could not merely tinker with laws and make piecemeal and ad hoc changes. Then, as now, the whole order of society needed changing. Its moral perception needed renewing. Its spiritual condition needed resurrecting. He once wrote: 'The strength of a country is most increased by its moral improvement and by the moral and religious instruction of its people.'

This 'Reformation of Manners' took up as much energy as his lifelong campaign against slavery. Thus, over and above the Society for Effecting the Abolition of the Slave Trade, he was involved in the Society for the Prevention of Cruelty to Animals, the Society for Suppression of Vice, the Church Mission Society and the Bible Society. He engaged in prison reform, opposed duelling, supported Sunday schools and campaigned to keep Sunday special, as we would say today. He campaigned for medical aid for the poor and education for the deaf, and supported campaigns to restrict capital punishment. He advocated legislation to improve the working conditions for chimney sweeps and textile workers, supported the creation of a free colony in Sierra Leone, helped engineer George III's 1787 Proclamation for the Discouragement of Vice as a remedy for the rising tide of immorality, and worked for (albeit rather limited) parliamentary reform.

The two causes that dominated Wilberforce's life – the abolition of the slave trade and the reformation of morality – may seem very different, but in Wilberforce's mind they shared one crucial factor: they were both moral and spiritual issues. All too often, looking for a new process or a new set of regulations is simply a substitute for accepting personal responsibility. We need to win our culture over to what we have always known, the kind of thing that Professor Michael Sandel, this year's Reith Lecturer, has been talking about – the idea that morality matters.

You cannot airbrush right and wrong out of the picture. Good and bad are not matters of opinion. We may legitimately debate about what exactly is good and what isn't, but at the end of the day, they are not merely topics for debate. Like Wilberforce, we need to grasp the liberating truth that humans are not simply cold, rational machines, but economic, spiritual and moral beings. Our humanity only flourishes when all three are honoured.

I believe we need a new moral spirit for our time, but first let us clear up some possible misunderstandings. By moral spirit I do not mean a narrowly angular, codified set of dos and don'ts censoriously applied by some new quango, like a committee on 'standards in public life'. It is not simply regulatory. It's not simply back to basics. Rather, it is reflective, it is relational, it is based on a sense of us, a sense – to quote a recent advert for a mobile phone company – that I am who I am because of everyone. We live in a community, I am not the sole arbiter of what is good.

Living dynamic relationships between me and other people – my family, friends, colleagues and local community – matter. At their root is the recognition that I owe you something because you are my neighbour. It is about a fundamental key shift from 'me' to 'we'; from judgements made purely selfishly to those made with the good of others in mind. This is the big mo (momentum if you are not a trader) of our times: a moral spirit that leads to enjoyment of life and its benefits when the driving attitude is not selfishness or greed.

This was expressed well by the Catholic Bishops' Conference of England and Wales in its 1996 report *The Common Good and the Catholic Church's Social Teaching*: 'Communities are brought into being by the participation of individual men and women, responding to this divine impulse towards social relationships – essentially, the impulse to love and to be loved – which was implanted by the God who created them.' Christians are encouraged to adopt a gracious, dynamic, spontaneous attitude that embraces responsibility and tries to avoid self-righteous proscriptions.

Of course we need laws and rules to restrain unacceptable behaviour. Human beings will never act in a way that makes laws unnecessary. But that is not to say that the only way forward is to create ever more laws. The moral spirit is about breaking free from the ethical straitjacket that regards ticking boxes as a moral panacea. It is about conscience making a comeback, about listening to what St Augustine once called 'the silent clamour of the heart'. It is about reuniting the economic with the moral and indeed the spiritual dimensions of being human.

Until recently, the idea that religion would play a significant role in such questions of public morality was an anathema to many, but this is no longer the case. As John Micklethwaite, the editor of *The Economist*, asserts in the title of his recent book: 'God is back' – although I have to say that as far as I am concerned he had never gone away. The bottom line is that we cannot today talk about public morality without talking about the religious dimension.

To be effective, morality needs to have an accepted authority. For Christians, Jews and Muslims, this authority derives from their belief in a monotheistic God who reveals these truths. This isn't to say that morality is the sole property of the religious, of course not. Whether we have religious beliefs or not, it is clear that we need to find common values for the common good if we are to live together in a community. For some, including myself, those common values will be rooted in and fed by their religious belief. The moral spirit will also be thoroughly informed by God. For others, that will not be the case, but this should not be a stumbling block. The moral spirit is integral to all of us, religious or not.

'Moral spirit' implies the acceptance of certain rules of living that contribute to the common good for all of us. And it implies doing so in a positive and humanising way, all the time working in a gracious manner that tries to avoid self-righteous proscriptions. The moral spirit is accessible to all, helpful to all and relevant to all. Without it, we cannot expect to flourish – either in our politics, our economics or our society.

For too long we have held to a vision of human nature in which human beings are independent, rational, morally autonomous, sovereign economic beings, exercising considered choice in such a way as to maximise their personal happiness. According to that vision, all we need to do is get the system right. If we do that we will all behave rationally and everything will be okay. The problem is that it simply doesn't work like that. In the first instance, humans are not simply calculating, rational creatures who work in that way. The Chartered Financial Analyst Institute recently conducted a survey that was apparently so astonishing it was given front-page treatment in the *Financial Times*. It found that most of its high-powered analysts believed that markets are not always rational, a belief that has formed the basis of efficient market theory for the past fifty years. More than 77 per cent of those polled disagreed with the prevailing consensus that investors behaved rationally.

This view that markets do not behave rationally but can be driven by human emotions is gaining credence as behavioural finance tries to grapple with the simple, almost forgotten, fact that flesh-and-blood humans drive our market economy – not detached, rationalist operatives. There is not so much a ghost in the market machine as a real, live human being. Echoing these sentiments, George Akerlof and Robert Shiller in their important new book *Animal Spirits* take the argument further. They make it clear that if we want to understand how economies work and how we can manage them and prosper, we must pay attention to the 'animal spirits': thought patterns that animate people's ideas and feelings.

They argue that economic crises such as the current financial and housing crisis are mainly caused by changing thought patterns, but that this fact goes against standard economic thinking. However, the crisis bears witness to the role of such changes in thinking. They conclude their introduction by saying:

> We see that animal spirits provide an easy answer to each of these questions. We also see that, correspondingly, none of these questions can be answered if people are viewed as having only economic motivations, which they pursue rationally – that is if the economy is seen as operating according to the invisible hand of Adam Smith.

We will never really understand important economic events unless we confront the fact that they are caused by such all too human things as temptation, envy, resentment and illusion. I suggest, however, that we need to go one step further and examine not only our gut instincts, our restless, inconsistent animal spirits that are at work in the economy; we need to acknowledge and work with a different and more defining human perspective, what I have called our moral spirit. Humans are more than just animals. We are moral and spiritual creatures, and if we fail to recognise that – either by pretending we are rational robots, or by pretending we are only animal spirits – we debase our humanity.

While there is undoubtedly an element of the animal instinct in humanity that governs our response to the world around us, there is also a common human bond, a collective notion of self-interested – but not selfish – morality that encourages us to pursue the common good. What these two lines of thought – the animal spirit and the moral spirit – have in common is the idea that the economy is not purely a rationalist silo, entire of itself, and run robotically by unaffected intelligences. The human dimension is crucial.

It has become fashionable in some circles to say that the goal of enjoying the benefits of financial reward while remaining responsive to the needs of others is either impossible or inherently contradictory. But I passionately believe that this is wrong. You can enjoy the benefits of financial reward while working with and for a moral spirit. Indeed, from the Christian point of view, the Parable of the Talents reminds us that it is a Christian duty to enhance service to others and to create wealth. Wilberforce himself recognised this, as did his influential contemporary Adam Smith, whose *Wealth of Nations* and *Theory of Moral Sentiments* went together. He understood that there is no inherent clash between creating wealth and living morally.

Quite the contrary, in fact. Serious wealth – meaning serious, sustainable, long-term, just wealth – demands morality. Wealth created without morality is unjust and unsustainable, as the recent financial disaster shows. Morality and economics should be inseparable and indivisible. Sadly, we seem to have forgotten this.

The last decade saw us creating a bewilderingly complex series of financial products that would satisfy all our – artificially stimulated –

demands. However, having assumed the role of creator, the financial institutions that manufactured these products out of nothing then refused to accept the moral responsibility that comes with the turf of being a creator. There was very little restraint in the quantum of credit that was created and very little responsibility for understanding the nature of these financial creations. It was assumed that, because humans are essentially rational, self-interest would be a sufficient regulator. We have seen the result.

Our economic thinking was drained of all traces of a moral spirit that would guide, regulate and control it. In our defence, we were certainly not the first society on earth to behave this way. Indeed, such behaviour, such willingness to sideline the moral spirit, is as old as the hills. The city of Tyre in Biblical times was shown by the prophet Ezekiel to be in precisely the same boat. This great Levantine city port was known as the chief trader and merchant to the world. It was Wall Street, or the City of London, or Beijing. Its worldwide trade made kings rich, its sharp intelligence made it world-wealthy. It worked good deals, used its head well, made a lot of money.

But the prophet spoke directly to the god-pretension of the city: 'Your heart is proud, going around saying, "I am a god" . . . A mere mortal, trying to be a god.' And the judgment on this powerful, fast-dealing, ever-growing demi-god was brutal: the balloon of their god-pretension was punctured. The city imploded. Overnight it lost its commanding importance as the centre of commerce. 'All who once knew you now throw up their hands. This can't have happened. This has happened!' (Ezekiel 28).

So our society was not the first to act in this way and I dare say we will not be the last. But that is no excuse for not now doing all we can to integrate the moral spirit into our financial and political practices, for trying to reunite *The Wealth of Nations* and *The Theory of Moral Sentiments*. A similar desire was echoed recently from an unusual source. In an interview with Lionel Barber, the editor of the *Financial Times*, the Chinese premier Wen Jiabao revealed that he carries with him in his briefcase Adam Smith's *Theory of Moral Sentiments* while on all his travels. Mr Wen said: 'Adam Smith made excellent arguments in his *Theory of Moral Sentiments* . . . if the fruits of a society's economic development cannot be shared by all, it is morally unsound and risky, as it is bound to jeopardise social stability. I think for quite some time this book has not attracted due attention.' It is a timely reminder for those of us in the West who have sought to divorce the moral spirit from our economic life.

Back in Wilberforce's time, the slave trade made up about 80 per cent of Great Britain's foreign income. This wealth was not widely shared, of course, and many British people did not gain anything personally from the trade except cheap sugar. However, a handful of individuals made fortunes, and there were significant vested interests at stake. The story behind this was the unpalatable fact that treating Africans as mere economic units of production rather than as human beings with personal, familial and community needs and desires was good business. On purely economic grounds – grounds that totally ignored the moral spirit – slavery made sense. No wonder Wilberforce and his fellow abolitionists 'endured great obloquy and opposition'.

Although the abolitionists did use economic arguments, just as they used political and cultural ones, there is no question that they fought their campaign primarily on moral and spiritual grounds. For them, no form of trade could ever be divorced from the underlying moral spirit. They belonged together. We would do well to remember this as we consider how the idea of a kind of disembodied amoral economics has come to shape our own time. Perhaps we, without realising it, have succumbed to the slavery of economics.

The economics of slavery may have been a thing of the past but the slavery of economics is very much of the present. There can be no doubting that, to quote another newspaper advertisement: 'We live in Financial Times'. According to the historian Niall Ferguson in his book *The Ascent of Money*, Planet Finance is beginning to dwarf Planet Earth. As we hardly need reminding, however, Planet Finance has hit a few difficulties. In the past year or so, stock markets have halved in value and more than thirty banks have gone bust or have been bailed out. This year the world economy is expected to shrink for the first time since the Second World War. It should not surprise us, then, that the recent crisis on Planet Finance has badly affected people on Planet Earth. According to the World Bank, an extra 53 million people will enter poverty this year, and according to Margaret Chan, director-general of the World Health Organization, an extra 200,000 to 400,000 children will die every year, because of the downturn. If that does not show that economics does exist outside morality, nothing does.

In reflecting on the financial crisis – and its huge human cost – we need to recognise that the causes are many and complex. We should take care in analysing the financial crisis that we do not reject out of hand the huge benefits reaped from the expanding economies of the past decade. Prosperity increased and hundreds of millions of people were taken out of extreme poverty through the increased creation of wealth. In the past sixteen years there were sixty-four quarters of consecutive economic growth. Too many people were lulled into a false sense of security, the sense that growth would continue in perpetuity and that the trees would grow to the skies. There were mistakes and failures by bankers, regulators, governments and central banks. Some pinpoint the blame on unsustainable levels of borrowing. Cheap borrowing led to a bubble in the housing market – in the UK house prices trebled between 1997 and 2007 – and consumers and companies built up huge debts. It has been estimated that households' and companies' debt amounted to 230 per cent of GDP.

This is undoubtedly true but it fails to recognise what underlies the huge debts. It's rather like blaming gin for the moral crisis against which Wilberforce so passionately campaigned. Of course, gin played its part – nasty, harmful, near-poisonous gin – but the real question was: why did so many people drank the stuff? Indeed, why did so many people get addicted to it?

Debt is the modern gin. Doubtless it has been available in toxic varieties, types of loan that would be unhealthy to take out in whatever quantity, but the key question is: why have people pursued it so single-mindedly? Why does Planet Finance dwarf Planet Earth and seemingly disregard Planet Humanity? The BBC's business editor, Robert Peston, has with acute insight identified seven 'poisonous dwarves' that contributed to the financial and banking crisis: complexity, opacity, connectedness, vested interests, ignorance, fraud and greed.

Interestingly the list begins with the systematic – problems with the complexity and opacity of products – but it doesn't end there. Fraud and greed are clearly moral (indeed, arguably spiritual) realities. Because we worked with a narrow, rationalistic idea of what it was to be human, downplaying the importance of the moral and spiritual in our decisions, those decisions became defective and topsy-turvy. Levels of personal borrowing soared. We borrowed more than we could afford, to consume what we did not require, to fulfil needs we did not have.

Debt came to be equity. Not only could banks lend prodigiously, and indeed irresponsibly, but the expansive growth of the private-equity industry was based on the entirely legitimate financial objective of 'debt is good' and its quantum restrained only by the willingness of a bank to lend with minimal restrictions. We confused debt with equity and came to the belief that financial engineering could give investments equity returns without equity risks. Financial judgements became devoid of any controlling ethical or spiritual discernment. You could hardly look for a better example of how we have ended up being long on knowledge but short on wisdom. The issue here – perhaps the one word that is equally at home in spiritual, moral, political and financial spheres – is 'trust'. Politicians know they cannot thrive without the trust of the electorate. Businesses can't prosper if their brand is not trusted, or if the relationship with their partners and suppliers is marked by mistrust. And theologians recognise that trust is a fundamental aspect of our human nature, essential in our relationships with one another and with God.

Not surprisingly what we have seen over recent months is a monumental breakdown in trust. At every level trust in financial institutions has been fractured, and it has been demonstrated beyond doubt that no economy, however robust, operates without trust. Shareholders question the roles of non-executive directors. Regulators believe they were let down by reporting from financial institutions. Depositors lost faith that their institutions would protect their savings. Small businesses believe they were left in the lurch by the withdrawal of credit facilities. And all that is without even mentioning Bernard Madoff and the remarkable way his scam was fuelled by the blind confidence that many smart professionals and intelligent celebrities had in the intermediaries investing their money, only to find themselves another dejected example of the global broken-trust phenomenon.

Financiers, for example, developed innovative instruments without questioning the moral issues regarding the valuations of these instruments. Morality seemed to have been contracted out. Relying on someone else became the new morality: a cunning way to avoid moral responsibility. At its most simple it is surely wrong not to know the value of a product being created. When no due diligence was needed, the products became detached from the issuing institutions and fuelled the insatiable aspirations of those peddling the underlying mortgages and credit opportunities.

Similarly, ethical commentators are marginalised and not really drawn into the financial mainstream. After all, financial judgements are self-contained and stand on their own; non-financial judgements are jumbled together as 'governance'. There is little understanding that the actions of fallible humans active in our economic system lie at the core of our crisis. Credit is not only trust, it is a promise. Like the Genesis creation story, credit is created ex nihilo by the fiat of the creator (a corporate board resolution). Hence ever greater levels of credit based on future promises could be brought into being. The assumption was that benign and stable conditions would underpin these promises, which by any standard were excessive.

The problem was that there was no restraint in the quantum of credit that was created and very little responsibility for understanding the nature of these financial creations. Banks created complex derivatives, structures, securitisations, default swaps, collaterised obligations. Unusually these creations are likely to outlive the creator and yet have the capacity when they unravel in the decades ahead to create even more financial chaos.

Credit default swaps, for example, have the perverse effect, as in the recent case of General Motors, of making the holders of these instruments more interested in the bankruptcy of the company than in its survival. This cannot be right.

Whereas in previous generations the credit officer was supreme in a financial institution, in the past ten years the head of syndications became the most valuable. It was to him that ultimately a financial institution could look to protect itself from the moral consequences of the products it had created. Destructive instruments could be passed on to someone else so that the creator institution never had to behold them. They were instead offloaded – syndicated – with relief to other unsuspecting players. The system caused wreckage, chaos and insecurity on a global scale. And it imploded under the weight of its own irresponsibility.

For too long, social and economic policy failed to recognise the significance of a broader context than the purely financial. Instead, it was driven by a narrow, even utilitarian, vision of what it is to be human. It reflected the sort of worldview evident in Charles Dickens's novel *Hard Times*, in which two alternative visions of human flourishing are presented. The utilitarian model of 'scientific political economy' is championed by Thomas Gradgrind, a hardware manufacturer, the founder of a model school and later MP for Coketown. The other vision is embodied by the people of Coketown, who are prone to a 'strange and unsavoury exuberance of imagination' and prefer reading novels to government statistics. 'In this life', Gradgrind insists, 'we want nothing but facts, sir; nothing but facts.'

Facts, numerics, research, quantitative analysis, indices, indicators: these have been our tools. Not values or wisdom. But 'facts', 'systems' and 'scientific political economics' are simply not enough. The moral and spiritual are not merely appendages to the basic 'economic human'. They are absolutely intrinsic to who we are, and critically important to our economies. Indeed they are the internal regulator of the economy, creating the moral compass we need in order to operate a successful market economy.

When the Queen visited the London School of Economics recently she asked about the financial crisis. 'If these things were so large, how come everyone missed them?' The head of the School of Management is said to have replied: 'At every stage someone was relying on someone else, and everyone thought they were doing the right things.' Everybody, it seems, had been playing pass the parcel, and they played it all the more energetically when they heard it starting to tick. Well, now it has exploded, and people – real, moral, spiritual people with jobs and homes and families – are suffering.

We need to pick up the pieces and put things back together again, but we cannot – we must not – go back to the status quo ante, the way things were before. We need to see the current financial – and indeed our political and social – crisis as an opportunity: an opportunity to build a better future, one that does not make the disastrous mistake of ignoring or silencing the moral spirit.

It will be clear from what I have said that when we ask what went wrong, we need to go beyond the obvious answers such as failure of regulation, mispriced assets, cheap money and excessive leverage. We need to recognise the deeper human roots of the problem. We need to win back our full humanity from the narrow and attenuated versions that have come to dominate both public policy and corporate finance. In short, we need to rehumanise the economy by reintroducing the moral spirit. In practice we need a process of repentance and reconciliation or, put in less theological language, remorse and resolution. However you describe it, this starts with the admission of error.

During the height of the financial crisis the then chairmen of three of the biggest banks 'fessed up and said sorry for their part in the crisis. We all remember them sitting before the select committee, like chastened schoolboys. A few months later, a similar thing happened regarding the expenses scandal. There was not – and has not yet been – any similarly official confession by representative politicians, but the number of informal ones has been too many to count. It soon became very clear to MPs that 'my claim was acceptable within the rules' simply wasn't going to wash. 'Within the rules' was not a good enough excuse. Those who wanted to keep their future in politics said sorry, said it loudly, and said it often. This is a positive sign.

'Sorry' is not a typical political or financial word. Such apologies from MPs and financial institutions indicated that those involved realised the crises were not simply political or financial ones. Trust had been broken, and forgiveness starts with confession. There could be no financial or political way out that did not recognise the basic human need to assuage the huge and righteous anger of the public and restore trust. Reconciliation was required. The nation has bayed for confession and – to some extent – it got it, but this is not the end.

Saying sorry is, as philosophers put it, a necessary but not sufficient cause. We also need repentance – not, as some atheists think, an antiquated and ritualistic gesture, but a serious desire to do things differently next time. In essence, we need to reinvest our economic, political, social thinking with the moral spirit. We need to create a new trust economy that recognises all the dimensions of the human person. We need to reshape the 'value drivers' of our society and find the language necessary to do so effectively and without embarrassment. In undertaking this task, we will not neglect the financial; we will, rather, put it in its proper place. We will direct the role it has to play in promoting human wellbeing.

As I have said, it is a Christian imperative to create value. Christ's parable of the talents makes it abundantly clear that we are to use our gifts to take intelligent risks and to create wealth, but we know from the rest of the New Testament that we are to do this morally, and for the good of others. The financial crisis has demonstrated that without these underlying values to drive it, the market economy cannot thrive and flourish. The market economy is a good servant but a bad master. Our task is to infuse the enterprise culture with a value system of honesty, integrity and the common good. Only that way will it truly flourish. So, let me suggest how we might start to go about that task.

Undoubtedly, we need to look at the regulatory framework. The law acts as an important control on human freedom. It restrains the worst excesses of human nature, and it is vital that any new framework takes that darker side of human nature seriously. Yet in doing so, the law must also recognise the limitations of its own role. Regulation in and of itself is never enough. Our social responsibility at work is not expressed by following the law. That is obligatory. A moral spirit is wider and more encompassing than narrow legalism. If we are to avoid the exponential increase in regulations affecting every aspect of our lives, we need to develop a spirit of personal responsibility.

In corporate terms we need to rethink how the boardroom works. We need more non-executive, independent voices on the boards of companies. Chosen principally on the basis of their experience and connectedness to the outside world, they can provide important links to the wider community. They can bring a broad understanding of the moral and spiritual dimensions of the issues being discussed and the decisions being taken. So we should invite teachers, voluntary-sector executives, military personnel, academics, members of the medical profession, journalists, commentators and other so-called 'outsiders' into our boardrooms. They will help us avoid some of the disastrous consequences of financial introspection.

For my part, at Lazard, I make sure I spend time with some of the younger people who work for me – not simply because I am inspired by their vitality, energy and intelligence, but because they are the equivalent for a modern bank of the shop floor. They know what's going on in a way that I, or other senior managers, never could. I find it very helpful to hear what they have to say about where the business is going and how it can be improved. Communication – in all sorts of directions – is a key part of building trust, of shaping, for the better, the moral spirit which is so important.

Beyond the boardroom, we need to encourage people to spend time with their colleagues and get to know them and their personal circumstances. I recently chaired a board meeting where we set aside the first half of the time to hear about the non-work aspects of people's lives – their concerns, interests and aspirations. That may sound twee and unfeasible in a hectic business world, but it is no less important for that. Crucially, over the long term, it builds up a sense of serious, meaningful and mutual relationships in the company, which, in turn, help the company flourish. Senior staff should connect with more junior staff. I am struck by the example of the German power company E.ON Ruhrgas. It randomly chooses groups of employees to meet on a bimonthly basis with members of the executive board to discuss key issues and to ensure that the board remains in touch with the grass roots.

The Chief Rabbi, Jonathan Sacks, wrote in *Faith in the Future*: 'Work has intrinsic value but only within a framework of other values. It is part of what it means to imitate God, but not all. There are other realities: the Sabbath world of rest, the festival world of celebration, and its house study with the service of the mind.' Work is critical, but it needs to be sensitive and responsive to our other commitments. Families are a key component of the civil society. However, these components are frequently put under enormous strain when parents are forced to work anti-social hours (especially weekends) or forced to spend days away from the family home, or when retailers use pester power to get their products sold to children. Again, this is where state (through regulation) and market (through sensitive and responsible employer practices) can come into play, by helping to foster the reformation of manners that we need to build a society that is responsive to human flourishing.

Similarly, businesses can build into their business models times for employees to pause and reflect – not simply respecting their desire for a holy day (whether that be a Friday, Saturday or Sunday) but by offering their employees incentives other than financial ones, such as enabling them to take parental leave, have flexible working arrangements, or even paid leave twice a year to enable their employees to volunteer.

Businesses have similar responsibilities to the community. As Marcus Agius, chairman of Barclays, put it in the *Telegraph* last December: 'Pulling back now [from community investment] should be unthinkable for reasons that go to the heart of the sort of business we all should try to be: one based on unchanging core values, one committed to building lasting relationships – with customers, employees, suppliers and our communities – and one able to take long-term decisions in what is a febrile short-term atmosphere.'

Another example is BauMax, an Austrian hardware retail store with strong Christian roots and ethics. BauMax has a strong emphasis on finding roles for handicapped workers in stores, initially those with physical disabilities and more recently people with mental problems. It also has a long-standing policy of donating tools to organisations for handicapped people who make products that BauMax sells in its stores. This awareness of the needs of especially vulnerable people in the vicinity of stores is exceptional but, in its own way, simply another example of the recognition that employees are people, and people live in, are made for, and only flourish through, relationship.

Recapturing a moral spirit to underpin our economy requires training, equipping and resourcing, and this needs to happen from an early age. Indeed, it needs to happen in the classroom. I am astonished by how little teaching there is in our schools and universities on the importance of the enterprise economy and the ethical underpinning required to ensure it functions in the best interests of the nation. As part of this moral training we need also to rediscover the significance of thrift. Thrift seldom gets a mention today. It is treated as if it were some antiquated old-school concept, quite irrelevant to modern living, but it is actually a key to our future prosperity. Individually and as a society, we need to learn to live within our means, and we need to get this message across as early as possible in our schools.

We need to see a revival of the moral spirit in the globalised context, too. It is an affront to the Christian conscience that we impose trade tariffs on the poorest countries seeking access to our markets while allowing free access – often subsidised – to the markets of the developing world for our products. A reform of the WTO is a pressing need of our time. If Wilberforce were with us today, I believe he would look to these unfair trade practices and the levels of extreme poverty in the world and spur us on to see this eliminated in our generation.

On the national level, injecting the moral spirit means finding ways of devolving power to the grass roots, to the people whose lives are most affected by the decisions taken – people running schools, hospitals and councils. Centralised command-and-control decision-making has become a prominent feature of our lives, but it denies the moral spirit and can be profoundly dehumanising. Support and training will be required to help people step up to the mark. As David Cameron so succinctly puts it, we can summarise this attitude in one word – 'responsible' – always realising that responsibility falls primarily upon our leaders.

We must look to civil society for the resources to help us. We applaud the media for uncovering the expenses issue, and there is a great opportunity for the media to take a lead in defining the character of our time. We can surely expect them to treat this movement to define a moral vision for life as authentic and important to our national life, not some God-slotted freak show. Our churches and other worshipping communities can play a critical role here. By renewing their mission of engagement with society, church leaders can help us recover the grammar of moral discourse that we all need.

Now is the time for the church to find its voice. Somehow it speaks in a tone so low as to be inaudible. The times are urgent and demand clear thought and leadership from those traditionally entrusted with giving moral leadership. It means participating fully in the public square. It means engaging in issues of public theology in way that is faithful, realistic and inspiring, in the way that the public theology think tank, Theos, has done so well over recent years.

This generation has, in the words of Os Guinness, too much to live with, and too little to live for. We are capable of extraordinary technological achievement and yet we struggle to answer the most basic of life's questions: Why am I here? What is it all for? We need to rediscover something to live for. Simply put, we need to recover a love of God and neighbour: to live at ease with God, at ease with our neighbours and at ease with ourselves. We need to look out to the world beyond ourselves, for there, in service to others, we will find our true humanity. We should find opportunities to benefit others – at home and abroad. We need to serve and give respect to others, and put their interests before our own. Nobody should believe that they are living a fulfilled life if they do not in some active way participate in voluntary action in the community. We have an extraordinary opportunity to forge a new character for the twenty-first century, but business can't go on as usual.

Fixing the character of our time will take courage. It will involve a reassertion of what it is to be truly human in the face of reductionist efforts to define people in economic terms alone. We need a vision of the common good that recognises what it is to be fully alive, one that recognises the moral spirit. It is the moral spirit that lies behind the idea that 'my word is my bond', the basic honesty that is absolutely fundamental to the functioning of a market economy. At heart, the moral spirit is the recognition that the relationships between me and my family, friends, colleagues, neighbours, community and environment matter.

The challenge is clear, and we have the resources to help us. We are empowered as no previous generation to make our voices heard in support of a new agenda. We can start today to articulate the basis for a new moral spirit that will rehumanise our social, political and economic structures and spur us on to create wealth, add value through our work, enjoy the benefits for taking risk and do so with a good conscience.

Wilberforce was undoubtedly an inspiring and epoch-changing man, and we could do with his like again today. But we don't need to – indeed, we mustn't – wait for another individual William Wilberforce. Together we can forge change. Rather, as he himself would have recognised, the responsibility lies on each and every one of us to help fix the character of the times.

Wilberforce and his fellow abolitionists created a movement that covered the length and breadth of the country gathering information, establishing contacts and building relationships for his cause. Today, each of us lives in a thoroughly interconnected world. We have the power of blogging, Twitter, Skype, email and the internet. All of these can be used to communicate an alternative narrative, a new point of view or new way of living well. The day of the digital 'little platoons' is here.

If we can seize the opportunity before us and embrace this new moral spirit, we could transform our times and restore hope to our society, and what Cowper said in tribute to Wilberforce will be true for us today. If we can indeed fix the character of our times, 'the better hour is near'.

APPENDIX

William Hague

2006 Conservative Party conference

Eleina, a Lithuanian girl, aged fifteen years, was offered a summer job by a family friend, selling ice cream in the UK. Excited by the prospect of seeing a new country and earning a good wage, she gratefully accepted. Within hours of landing at Heathrow she had her passport taken from her and was sold to a people-trafficking gang for £4,000. She was taken to Birmingham by an Albanian gang member, raped and forced to work as a prostitute in a brothel – just two days after arriving in Britain. A few months later, she was bought for £3,000, transported to Coventry, repeatedly violated and forced to sell her body. Within days she was traded again, herded between four different owners in London, and then purchased by a man for £1,500 in Sheffield. She eventually managed to escape by running barefoot to a police station, having been sold seven times in just three months, her price decreasing with each new owner. When finally back in Lithuania she said of her ordeal: 'I have run out of tears . . . I try to forget but sometimes I have nightmares about it.'

Eleina's 'nightmare' graphically illustrates the tragic and unimaginable suffering of many victims of human trafficking as they are sold for thousands of pounds, and passed through chains of unscrupulous traders. I first began to learn about new forms of slavery when asked to speak on this subject in January 2005. I soon discovered that from the villages of Africa to the farms, sweatshops and brothels of south Asia and the Indian subcontinent, slavery still flourishes. Slaves harvest cocoa and other crops in Ivory Coast, mine diamonds in Sierra Leone and are forced into domestic servitude in Latin America. In addition, hundreds of young children are kidnapped each year and forced to become soldiers for rebel fighters in war zones such as Liberia and the Congo. But this kind of exploitation is not exclusive to the developing world.

Closer to home slavery lies further below the surface, but is there nonetheless. People are trafficked from country to country within Europe, undetected by state authorities, as part of a thriving and profitable trade, but one which deals in the same misery as more traditional forms of slavery. I read about intricate networks of approachers, transporters, middlemen, storehouses and trafficking routes, and encountered heartrending accounts by the victims themselves. The scale of the problem is, undeniably, huge. A recent report from the UN Office of Drugs and Crime concludes that no country in the entire world is immune to human trafficking, be it as a country of origin, destination or transit. After narcotics, it equals arms-dealing as the second largest criminal industry in the world and is the fastest growing. It is closely connected with other illegal activities such as money-laundering, drug-trafficking and document forgery and is estimated by the FBI to generate around $9.5 billion a year in revenue. On a human scale the statistics are worse still. Approximately 600,000 to 800,000 men, women and children are trafficked across international borders each year; 80 per cent are women and girls, while 50 per cent are children.

The most common practice in Europe is in the trafficking of young girls and women for the purpose of sexual exploitation.

Other victims are forced into productive labour, or used for other purposes such as benefit fraud and organ donation. Pregnant women are highly prized as their babies can be bought and sold for thousands of pounds in the developed world.

Human trafficking is an industry that uses a variety of cruel methods and practices. Many victims start their journeys by falling casualty to the deceit of seemingly respectable individuals who offer work and opportunity in far-off places. They travel of their own free will to the promised destination only to find that lying in wait are organised criminal gangs ready to exploit them. Violence and intimidation are frequently used to control victims in environments where they find themselves cut off from the protection of family members and community, language and culture, many miles from home.

So, why is human trafficking, in all its forms, on the increase? One reason is globalisation. Economic barriers have fallen. Borders have become more porous. Travel has become cheaper and technology more advanced. We have greater mobility and freedom than ever before, resulting in exceptionally diverse, fluid and fast-moving labour markets. This provides the environment necessary for criminal organisations to run networks of human traffic across national boundaries, to unprecedented levels.

In Europe, the tearing down of the Iron Curtain, along with the expansion of the EU, has further increased this labour mobility; it is easier to cross national boundaries either legitimately or illegally. As the disparities between developing and developed countries increase, market forces draw workers long distances to benefit from the great differentials in wages compared with those at home. War and conflict across many parts of the world have also created a large pool of displaced people. Individuals are thus willing to travel great distances in search of opportunity at considerable personal risk; not least from the criminal gangs who wish to exploit the same market openings.

As Moises Naim, editor of *Foreign Policy* magazine, comments in his book *Illicit*: 'Smuggling is no longer what crooks do between two countries across borders. Now we are talking about large, wealthy, ruthless, global, agile networks that are undermining governance, democracy and governmental functioning in many countries.'

Having examined the magnitude of the problem before us, it would help to reflect upon the extraordinary achievements of William Wilberforce who, 200 years ago, led and eventually won the moral argument to outlaw the slave trade in Britain, despite powerful economic and political opposition. We can then draw an obvious parallel with the situation we find today. The strength of commercial opposition faced by Wilberforce betrayed the levels of unscrupulous profit that were made in the nineteenth century from enslaving others. We may conclude that these powerful economic forces have always existed, to a greater or lesser extent ever since, and indeed have grown stronger in recent years as market opportunities have increased. In the twenty-first century, just as in the eighteenth and nineteenth, moral revulsion can mobilise public opinion, but now we are fighting slavery in a different form. This is a trade which is illegal, underground and has the potential to weaken governments and the rule of law. To reduce the trade in human beings we must disrupt the market forces of demand and supply: make the rewards less lucrative, increase the risks of capture and reduce the demand.

Since early 2005, the government has been proactive in its attempt to combat human trafficking. It established a Ministerial Group on Human Trafficking to co-ordinate and ensure cross-departmental policy, and produced a public consultation paper in January 2006 with a national action plan to be published towards the end of this year.

It also launched Operation Pentameter, a successful three-month project to tackle trafficking for sexual exploitation involving all fifty-five police forces across the UK. The programme led to the rescue of eighty-four trafficked women (twelve of whom were, shockingly, aged between fourteen and seventeen years), and 232 people were arrested. A UK Human Trafficking Centre will be established this autumn to support, develop, co-ordinate and deliver the UK's policing response to trafficking in human beings.

All these initiatives are to be welcomed, but in the meantime the problem of human trafficking into the UK has shown no sign of improvement and, worryingly, appears to have got worse. Cases have been documented in Britain's biggest cities, rural towns and quiet suburbs. It seems no area is unaffected. This evening, I would like to focus on a few things which we could do to remedy the situation.

First, more research is required to understand the nature of the problem in the UK. What is it that makes our country, alongside countries such as Germany and Italy, a primary destination in Europe for traffickers? Are criminal sentences an inadequate deterrent, the odds of detection too low, the conviction rates too poor, or the demand for services too high? Or is it a combination of all these factors? Due to the subversive nature of the crime, it is difficult to calculate how many people have been trafficked to the UK, but it should be possible to compile more accurate data than we have at present. A comprehensive and independent research report on the extent of human trafficking must be undertaken.

In terms of reducing the supply side of trafficking, we must act to decrease the profits and increase the risks for traffickers. Combating supply must be embedded in policing priorities, with the impetus coming from the very top and filtering down to all levels of law enforcement. Those working on the ground must be given the tools and support they need, operating in conjunction with other legal agencies and victim support groups.

Due to the international dimension of trafficking, we must ensure that there is greater co-operation between our government and police force with those from overseas – especially countries of origin.

Recently, the Albanian and Greek governments have pledged to address child-trafficking between their countries, with the objective of returning child victims to Albania.

Many source countries lack the judicial infrastructure and law enforcement capacity to stem the trade. In these cases, sharing expertise in areas such as police training and intelligence-gathering, and techniques to fight organised crime, is vital. For example, in April the Australian federal police signed an agreement with the Vietnamese national police force to tackle human trafficking and other transnational criminal activity. Within Europe, pressure can also be brought to bear on countries wishing to join the EU, with the effectiveness of law enforcement measures made a strict criterion for entry.

Another aspect of reducing supply is to educate, empower and protect vulnerable individuals within source countries. For example, last year, Austrian embassies and consulates in Russia, Belarus and Ukraine began issuing special information about the dangers of forced prostitution to women who applied for visas intending to work in locations that are deemed to be at risk from criminal activity. The women are also required to apply for visas in person. Information programmes can be implemented at very little cost with considerable benefit: two years ago the Estonian government sponsored an essay-writing competition for young people titled 'How could I fall into the hands of traffickers?' Elsewhere, the government of Bangladesh has distributed anti-trafficking material to members of micro-lending schemes. This demonstrates the valuable relationship between anti-trafficking campaigns and broader economic and social development projects in developing countries.

Governments instinctively rely on the usual and most readily available tools they have at their disposal to tackle human trafficking: protecting national borders and law enforcement. But human trafficking must not be viewed solely as organised immigration crime. It is much more complex than that. Many victims travel to the UK with their own passports, which are then seized by the traffickers upon arrival.

Curbing demand is just as crucial, if not more so in the long term. But it requires informing, educating and persuading both consumers and employers in both legal and illegal markets, where slave labour is used. In the UK, Operation Pentameter sent out campaign letters giving advice on how to recognise a trafficked woman and the immorality of sleeping with one to men's magazines. Leaflets were also handed out to men going to the World Cup. In Australia they have gone further: the federal police are running a campaign to encourage people who purchase sexual services to call a special hotline number anonymously if they believe any women they have come across are being forced to work as prostitutes.

Businesses should be encouraged to adopt fair trade practices which ban the use of slave labour and the public should be encouraged to buy these products. Purchasing fairly traded chocolate bars and other food items and ethically produced clothing and goods are small ways in which we can all make a difference.

Finally, a great deal needs to be done in terms of victim protection. According to the US State Department's Trafficking in Persons Report 2006, 'there is no specialised immigration status available for trafficking victims and shelter capacity for victims continued to be limited'. The government has not signed the Council of Europe's Convention on Action against the Trafficking in Human Beings, which provides victims with a thirty-day reflection period, arguing that it might act as 'a pull factor' to the UK and thus encourage illegal immigration. The Home Office has said it is 'hoping to make a decision on signature in the course of developing the National Action Plan on Trafficking' and we await the outcome. We would like to see its assumptions and the basis of its eventual pronouncement so we too can assess whether this is the right choice.

There are no free specialised helplines for victims to call, and currently the UK has only one government scheme, the Poppy Project, providing safe accommodation for twenty-five females who have been trafficked for sexual exploitation. Partnering with NGOs and charities is a more effective way of providing such services. For example, the state of São Paulo has worked with a local NGO to establish a victim support centre near the city's airport and gives information about government protection and legal procedures.

Another good example is the Rescue and Restore campaign, which identifies and assists victims in the US through national and local coalitions of civic groups, NGOs and faith-based organisations. A central helpline provides support to enable these groups to recognise cases of human trafficking and connects victims to approved NGOs in their local area. In terms of financing assistance schemes, the state of Baden-Württemberg in Germany has a straightforward approach: traffickers' assets are confiscated and used to fund future investigations and rehabilitation programmes.

The policies I have mentioned are just a few ideas on how the market forces of supply and demand can be obstructed. They reflect the breadth of measures that are available and required, domestically and internationally, to tackle a criminal activity that is growing both in volume and complexity.

As we seek to combine Conservatism with compassion in a practical way, Wilberforce's example is one we should follow. The challenges we face are different but we carry the responsibility to uphold and protect the moral legacy that he, and others, laid down for us. I have already spoken of the strong forces in today's world that allow trafficking to flourish. A strong international coalition is therefore required with the joint forces of governments, businesses, activists, the media, charities and faith-based organisations all working alongside one another. Efforts to build such a coalition are already underway, exemplified in the excellent work of Steve

Chalke and Stop the Traffik. I fully support their campaign and look forward to hearing more details later.

Slavery is still found in every corner of the globe, under many different guises, and employs all kinds of deceitful and violent methods to subjugate people for profit. The task for us all is to ensure that we do not ignore an age-old problem that sometimes lies out of sight, but nevertheless still blights the lives of many thousands of vulnerable people in this country and around the world. We need to ask ourselves whether we have the political will, as Wilberforce did, to eradicate it. I hope that the answer is yes.